Contents

KU-050-515

05/07

UNIVERSITY OF
WOLVERHAMPTON

Harrison Learning Centre
City Campus
University of Wolverhampton
St Peter's Square
Wolverhampton
WV1 1RH
Telephone: 0845 408 1631
Online renewals:
www.wlv.ac.uk/lib/myaccount

Telephone Renewals: 01902 321333 or 0845 408 1631
Please RETURN this item on or before the last date shown above.
Fines will be charged if items are returned late.
See tariff of fines displayed at the Counter.   (L2)

In easy steps is an imprint of In Easy Steps Limited
4 Chapel Court · 42 Holly Walk · Leamington Spa
Warwickshire · United Kingdom · CV32 4YS
www.ineasysteps.com

Notice of Liability
Every effort has been made to ensure that this book contains accurate
and current information. However, In Easy Steps Limited and the
author shall not be liable for any loss or damage suffered by readers
as a result of any information contained herein.

Trademarks
All trademarks are acknowledged as belonging to their respective
companies.

In Easy Steps Limited supports The Forest Stewardship Council (FSC),
the leading international forest certification organisation. All our titles
that are printed on Greenpeace approved FSC certified paper carry the
FSC logo.

MIX
Paper from
responsible sources
FSC® C020837

Printed and bound in the United Kingdom

ISBN 978-1-84078-541-8

Foreword

The creation of this book has been for me, Mike McGrath, an exciting personal journey in discovering how CSS3 can really be implemented in today's web browsers. It has been fascinating to determine exactly which parts of the various modules of the CSS3 specifications are currently supported by Internet Explorer, Firefox, Google Chrome, Safari, and Opera. The "Handy Reference" section at the end of the book lists the current working CSS3 properties. All the examples I have given in this book demonstrate CSS3 features that are presently supported by leading web browsers and the screenshots illustrate the actual results produced by the listed code. I truly believe that now, more than ever, authors can integrate CSS3 presentation with JavaScript functionality and HTML5 document structure to produce stunning interactive web pages.

Conventions in this book

In order to clarify the code listed in the steps given in each example I have adopted certain colorization conventions. CSS selectors are colored blue, like this:

div#box > p

CSS properties and punctuation are also colored blue, but specified values are colored red:

{ color : red ; background : yellow }

CSS comments are colored green:

/* Validated by W3C CSS Validation Service */

HTML document content and markup tags are simply colored black:

<title>HTML5 in easy steps</title>

Additionally, in order to identify each source code file described in the steps a colored icon and the file name appears in the margin alongside the steps, such as these:

style.css   page.html   data.xml   image.png

The source code of HTML documents used in the book's examples is not listed in full to avoid unnecessary repetition but the listed HTML code is the entire fragment of the document, including markup tags, to which the listed CSS code is applied.

Grabbing the source code

For convenience I have placed all the source code files and associated files featured in this book into a single ZIP archive file. This contains all CSS style sheets, HTML documents, and image files used by the examples. You can obtain the complete archive by following these easy steps:

1 Browse to **http://www.ineasysteps.com**, then navigate to "Free Resources" and choose the "Downloads" section

2 Find "CSS3 in easy steps" in the list, then click on the hyperlink entitled "All Code Examples" to download the archive

3 Now extract the archive contents to any convenient location on your computer

Undoubtedly CSS3 provides significant new creative possibilities in web page authoring – as this book's examples demonstrate. I sincerely hope you enjoy discovering how CSS3 can be used to create stunning interactive web pages in today's latest web browsers as much as I did.

Mike McGrath

1 Getting started

Welcome to the exciting world of Cascading Style Sheets (CSS). This chapter demonstrates the various ways in which styles can be applied to HTML elements.

Introducing CSS

Cascading Style Sheets (CSS) is a language used to control the presentation of elements within HyperText Markup Language (HTML) documents. Presentation is specified by "styles" that may be assigned "inline" to HTML element **style** attributes, or by "rules" within **<style> </style>** tags in the HTML document's head section, or as rules within separate style sheets. Each style rule selects specified elements then applies specified styles to them.

CSS was created by the World Wide Web Consortium (W3C) to regain control of document markup as HTML grew from the initial few "tags" that merely defined the structural elements of a document – headings, paragraphs, hyperlinks, and lists. As further tags were added controlling images, text color, font size, and background color, it became recognized that the source code of many web pages often contained a great deal of markup for very little actual content.

The W3C offered a solution to regain control of document markup by separating their structural and presentational aspects. HTML tags would continue to control the structure but presentational aspects would now be contolled by "style rules" written in the Cascading Style Sheet (CSS) language. Besides distinguishing between structural and presentational aspects of a document, the CSS solution brings these additional benefits:

- **Easier maintenance** – a single style sheet can control multiple HTML documents, so changing appearance across an entire website is possible by editing just one style sheet

- **Smaller file sizes** – removal of all presentational markup from HTML produces smaller files, which download faster

- **Greater control** – margins, borders, padding, background color, and background images to any HTML element, and the appearance of certain parts of the interface, such as the cursor, can now be specified

The CSS level 3 specification (CSS3) is divided into modules that allow enhancements such as rounded borders, drop-shadows, gradient color-fills, and animation effects – these and more are demonstrated by example in this book.

Sir Tim Berners Lee, W3C Director and inventor of the World Wide Web

W3C®

The W3C is an international consortium whose members work together to develop web standards. The CSS home page can be found on the W3C website at **www.w3.org/Style/CSS**

Understanding the cascade

The term "Cascading" in CSS describes the manner in which style rules can fall from one style sheet to another. The cascade determines which style rule will have precedence over others and be the one applied to the selected HTML element.

There are three basic types of style sheet that can specify style rules to be applied to HTML elements:

- **Browser (default) style sheet** – browsers employ an intrinsic set of style rules that they apply to all web pages by default. These vary slightly between different browsers but all have common features, such as black text and blue hyperlinks

- **User style sheet** – most browsers allow the user to specify their own appearance preferences, which effectively creates a custom style sheet that overrides the browser's default style sheet

- **Author style sheet** – where the HTML document specifies a style sheet created by the web page author the browser will apply the style rules it contains, overriding both the user style sheet and the default browser style sheet

Hot tip

There are other style sheet languages, such as the eXtensible Stylesheet Language (XSL), but CSS is by far the most popular style sheet language.

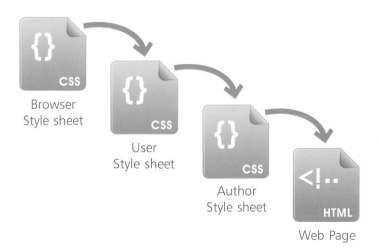

Browser Style sheet

User Style sheet

Author Style sheet

Web Page

So the cascade means that the browser will typically apply the style rules in an author style sheet, if present. Otherwise it will apply the style rules in a user style sheet, if present. Otherwise it will apply the style rules in the browser's style sheet by default.

Creating style rules

In CSS each style rule is comprised of TWO main parts:

● **Selector** – specifying which element/s of the HTML document are the target of that rule

● **Declaration Block** – specifying how properties of the selected target element should be styled

A style rule (or "style rule set") begins with the selector, followed by the declaration block within a pair of curly brackets (braces). The braces contain one or more declarations that each specify a property and a valid value for that property, as in this example:

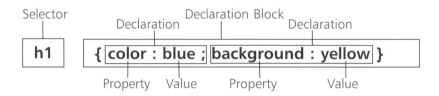

Typically the selector targets (selects) a particular HTML element for styling – such as all **<h1>** heading elements in the document using the style rule set example above.

The declaration block in the example above contains two declarations to determine the foreground and background colors of the selected target elements. The CSS **color** property is assigned a **blue** value – so each **<h1>** heading element will have blue foreground text. Similarly, the CSS **background** property is assigned a **yellow** value – so each **<h1>** heading element will have a yellow background.

Notice how the CSS declaration uses a : colon character to assign a value to a property. Notice also that it requires the declarations to be separated by a ; semi-colon character.

The final declaration in the declaration block does not need to be terminated by a semi-colon. However, some web page authors prefer to habitually terminate all CSS declarations so they need not remember to add a separating semi-colon when adding further declarations to an existing style rule set.

Don't forget

In conformance with the CSS specifications, the examples listed throughout this book do not add a semi-colon terminator after the final declaration in a declaration block.

1 When creating a new CSS style rule the author must initially specify a selector to target the HTML element to which the rule will be applied – strictly speaking, the CSS selector is everything that appears before the opening brace of the declaration block
h1

2 Next the declaration block must be created by adding a pair of braces after the selector
h1 {   }

3 Now a declaration can be inserted within the declaration block to assign a value to a property
h1 { color : blue }

4 A second declaration can then be added within the declaration block, separated from the first by a semi-colon
h1 { color : blue ; background : yellow }

5 The style rule set is now complete but can also be applied to another HTML element by extending the selector to become a comma-separated list
h1, h2 { color : blue ; background : yellow }

6 Further style rule sets can then be added below the first style rule set to target other elements
h1, h2   { color : blue ; background : yellow }
p   { color : red }

Hot tip

Whitespace (spaces, tabs, line feeds, and carriage returns) is permitted within style rule sets to allow the author to format the style rules to their own preference. Typically style rule sets with fewer than four declarations are written on a single line, otherwise they are written across multiple lines for clarity.

13

Applying internal style rules

A style sheet is simply a collection of style rule sets to be applied to an HTML document. An internal style sheet can be created by inserting the style rule sets between **<style>** and **</style>** tags in the head section of the HTML document. The opening **<style>** tag should include a **type** attribute assigned a MIME type of "text/css" to describe the style sheet as using the CSS language. Optionally, this tag may also include a **media** attribute assigned a "screen" value to specifically describe the viewing medium as a color computer screen – although this is the default value if the **media** attribute is omitted.

All modern web browsers support CSS but if you wish to hide the internal style sheet from older browers the style rule sets can be enclosed within **<!--** and **-->** HTML comment tags.

Hot tip

MIME (Multipart Internet Mail Extension) types describe file types – **text/html** for HTML files, **text/javascript** for scripts, **text/css** for style sheets.

internal.html

1. Create an HTML5 document containing heading, sub-heading, and paragraph elements

```html
<!DOCTYPE HTML>
<html lang="en">
<head>
<meta charset="UTF-8">
<title>Internal style rules</title>
</head>
<body>
<h1>Heading styled by CSS</h1>
<h2>Sub-heading styled by CSS</h2>
<p>Paragraph styled by CSS</p>
</body>
</html>
```

2. In the head section of the document, immediately after the closing **</title>** tag, insert a style element block containing style rule sets for each content element

```css
<style type="text/css" media="screen">
<!--
h1      { color : blue ; background : yellow }
h2      { color : white ; background : green }
p       { color : red }
-->
</style>
```

3. Save the HTML file then open it in a web browser to see the styles applied to the content elements

Style rules can also be applied internally to individual HTML elements by assigning "inline" properties and values to the **style** attribute of that element. This will override the rules applicable to the same properties of that element that may have been specified in any other style sheet.

4   Edit the heading elements to reverse the colors specified in the style sheet within the document's head section

```
<h1 style="color : yellow ; background : blue">
                        Heading styled by CSS</h1>
<h2 style="color : green ; background : white">
                        Sub-heading styled by CSS</h2>
```

5   Save the HTML file again then re-open it in a web browser to see the previous styles get overridden

Don't forget

Internal style sheets should only be used where it is desirable to create a single HTML document for portability – external style sheets, described overleaf, are always preferable.

15

Beware

The use of inline style rules should be avoided at all costs – always place style rules within a style sheet instead.

Although described here for completeness there are drawbacks to using internal style rules. Multiple individual inline styles are more difficult to maintain than a single style rule in a style sheet as they would need to be individually altered to affect a style change to a number of elements. An internal style sheet is only applicable to the HTML document in which it is contained, whereas an external style sheet can apply to multiple web pages to consistently style an entire website from a single file.

Linking an external style sheet

An external style sheet style is simply a collection of style rule sets listed in a plain text file, such as those created by Windows' Notepad application, then saved with a ".css" file extension. The style sheet can then be linked to HTML documents using a **<link>** tag. This must include a **type** attribute assigned a MIME type of "text/css" to denote using the CSS language, a **rel** attribute assigned a "stylesheet" relationship value, and an **href** attribute assigned the path to the style sheet file. Optionally, this tag may also include a **media** attribute assigned a "screen" value to describe the viewing medium as a color computer screen – although this is the default value if the **media** attribute is omitted.

external-1.html

external-2.html

1 Create two HTML documents containing heading and paragraph elements
```
<!DOCTYPE HTML>
<html lang="en">
<head>
<meta charset="UTF-8">
<title>External style rules</title>
</head>
<body>
<h1>Heading styled by CSS</h1>
<p>Paragraph styled by CSS</p>
</body>
</html>
```

2 In the head section of each HTML document, immediately after the closing **</title>** tag, insert a link element specifying a style sheet to be used
```
<link type="text/css"
     rel="stylesheet" href="external.css" media="screen">
```

external.css

3 Save the HTML files then open a plain text editor, such as Notepad, and list style rule sets for content elements
```
h1 { color : blue ; background : yellow }
p  { color : red ; background : white }
```

4 Save the CSS file alongside the HTML files, named as "external.css", then open the HTML files in a web browser to see the styles applied to each web page

16

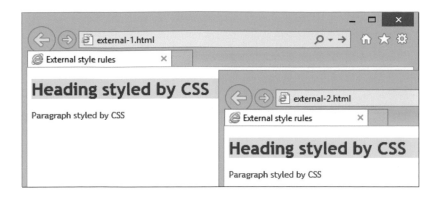

Single line or multi-line comments can be added to CSS style sheets between /* and */ characters. These are ignored by web browsers but are useful to describe aspects of the style sheet.

5   Re-open the style sheet file in a plain text editor and insert a commented title at the very start of the file
    `/* Master Style Sheet for external-x.html Pages */`

6   Now edit the style rule sets to reverse the previous colors
    `h1 { color : yellow ; background : blue }`
    `p  { color : white ; background : red }`

7   Save the style sheet file once more then re-open (or refresh) each HTML page in a web browser to see modified style rules applied to both web pages

Hot tip

CSS comments can appear both outside and within rule sets – so can be used to "comment-out" entire rules or individual declarations.

Don't forget

Always use external style sheets rather than internal style sheets or inline style rules – to cleanly separate the structural and presentational aspects of web pages.

17

Importing other style sheets

Multiple external style sheets can be used to control different aspects of HTML documents using **@import** directives to specify the path to each CSS file. These must be placed before any other rules in the style sheet and be terminated by a semi-colon.

import.html

1 Create an HTML document containing heading and paragraph elements

```
<!DOCTYPE HTML>
<html lang="en">
<head>
<meta charset="UTF-8">
<title>Importing style sheets</title>
</head>
<body>
<h1>Heading styled by CSS</h1>
<h2>Sub-heading styled by CSS</h2>
<p>Paragraph styled by CSS</p>
</body>
</html>
```

2 In the head section of the HTML document, immediately after the closing **</title>** tag, insert a link to a "master" style sheet

```
<link type="text/css"
      rel="stylesheet" href="import.css" media="screen">
```

import.css

3 Save the HTML file then open a plain text editor and create the "master" style sheet that simply imports two other style sheets to style the headings and paragraphs within the web page

```
@import "headings.css" ;
@import "paragraphs.css" ;
```

paragraphs.css

4 Save the master style sheet as "import.css" alongside the HTML file then create a style sheet to specify the appearance of paragraphs

```
p { color : blue }
p:first-letter { font-size : xx-large }
```

headings.css

5 Save the second style sheet as "paragraphs.css" alongside the HTML file then create another style sheet to specify the appearance of headings

```
h1 { color : red ; font-family : "Script", cursive }
h2 { color : green }
```

6 Save the third style sheet as "headings.css" alongside the HTML file then open the web page in a browser to see the content elements styled by the style sheets imported via the master style sheet

7 Edit the "headings.css" style sheet to match all heading colors to the paragraph color then refresh the browser to see the changes
h1 { color : blue ; font-family : "Segoe Script", cursive }
h2 { color : blue }

Summary

- CSS is a language provided by the W3C to regain control of markup by separating document structure from presentation

- The cascade allows style rules to fall from one style sheet to another and determines which style rule will be applied

- Each style rule comprises of a selector and a declaration block

- Each declaration specifies a property and a value to be applied to that property, separated by a : colon character

- A style rule set contains multiple declarations, each separated from the next by a ; semi-colon character

- The final declaration in a declaration block need not be terminated with a ; semi-colon character

- An internal style sheet is a collection of style rules contained within **<style>** tags in the head section of an HTML document

- Style rules can also be applied inline by assigning properties and values to the **style** attribute of an HTML element

- Inline style rules are difficult to maintain and should be avoided

- External style sheets are recommended to cleanly separate structure and presentation – internal style sheets should only be created in special circumstances

- An external style sheet is a collection of style rule sets listed in a plain text file saved with a **.css** file extension

- An HTML document can link an external style sheet file by adding a **<link>** element in the document's head section

- Each **<link>** element must contain **rel**, **type**, and **href** attributes

- The MIME type of CSS is **text/css**

- All **@import** directives must appear before other rules in a style sheet and must be terminated with a ; semi-colon character

2 Selecting targets

This chapter demonstrates all the different ways in which HTML elements can be selected for styling in CSS.

Selecting by element type

The selector part of a style rule selects elements in an HTML document to be styled according to the values specified in that rule's Declaration Block.

A "type" selector selects all elements in the page that match the selector. Multiple elements can be selected by a type selector that specifies a comma-separated list of element types.

type.html

type.css

1   Create an HTML document containing a heading and an unordered list of hyperlinks within a "div" container
```
<div>
<h1>Large Heading</h1>
<ul>
<li><a href="www.google.com">Google</a></li>
<li><a href="www.yahoo.com">Yahoo</a></li>
<li><a href="www.mediafire.com">MediaFire</a></li>
</ul>
</div>
```

2   Create a linked style sheet with a style rule setting the width of the container element
```
div { width : 50% }
```

3   Add a style rule setting the background color of all hyperlinks
```
a { background : yellow }
```

4   Now add a style rule setting the background color of both the heading and list elements
```
h1, ul { background : aqua }
```

5   Save the style sheet file alongside the HTML file then open the web page in a browser to see the elements styled by type selectors

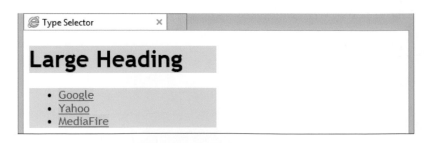

…cont'd

The CSS * universal selector can be used to select elements of all types within an HTML document – as if it was a selector listing all element types as a comma-separated list.

6. Edit the style sheet by adding a style rule with a universal selector to make all text italic
* { font-style : italic }

7. Save the amended style sheet then refresh the browser to see both heading and list text become italic

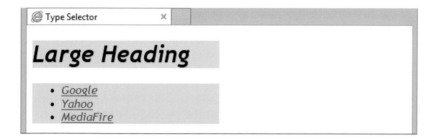

The * universal selector can also be used to select elements of any type contained within a specified element type.

8. Edit the style sheet by adding a style rule with a universal selector to add a border around all elements within the "div" container
div * { border : 0.2em solid red }

9. Save the amended style sheet then refresh the browser once more to see borders added around the elements

Beware

Remember that there must be a comma between the element types in a selector targeting multiple element types.

23

Don't forget

The **div *** selector selects elements of all types within the div container, but not the **<div>** element itself.

Selecting by class

As an alternative to selecting elements by type, a class selector can select HTML elements that contain a **class** attribute that has been assigned a value matching the selector. The class selector begins with a . period character followed by the class value to match. This is especially useful to apply the style rule across a number of specific elements of different type.

Additionally a class selector can be combined with a type selector to select specific instances of a class. In this case the selector first specifies the element type, followed by a period character and the class value to match.

class.html)

 Create an HTML document containing a paragraph including two spanned words, in which all elements have a common class value
<p class="frame">You can fool all the people <span class="frame">some</span> of the time, and <span class="frame">some</span> of the people all the time, but you cannot fool all the people all of the time.</p>

class.css

 Create a linked style sheet with a style rule drawing red borders around each element using the class value
.frame { border : 0.2em solid red }

 Now add a rule overriding the previous one for the paragraph element only, to draw a blue border around the paragraph and set its width
p.frame { border : 0.2em solid blue ; width : 50% }

 Save the style sheet file alongside the HTML document then open the web page in a browser to see the elements styled by the class selectors

Don't forget

Other paragraphs added to this HTML document would not be styled with this style sheet – unless they too contained a class attribute with the value of "frame".

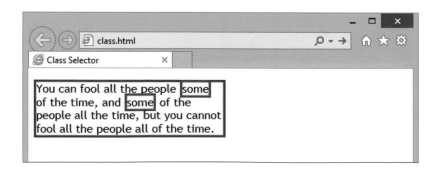

24

Selecting by identity

Similar to a class selector, an ID selector can select HTML elements that contain an **id** attribute that has been assigned a value matching the selector. The ID selector begins with a **#** hash character followed by the ID value to match. This is mostly useful to apply the style rule to one specific element as each **id** attribute value must be unique within the HTML document.

Optionally an ID selector can be combined with a type selector simply to identify the element type. In this case the selector first specifies the element type, followed by a hash character and the ID value to match.

1 Create an HTML document containing a paragraph including two spanned phrases, in which all elements have a unique ID value
```
<p id="para1">You may only be someone
<span id="span1">in the world</span><br>
but to someone else you may
<span id="span2">be the world</span></p>
```

id.html

2 Create a linked style sheet with style rules painting colored backgrounds behind the text in each span element
```
#span1 { background : yellow }
#span2 { background : lime }
```

id.css

3 Now add a style rule to paint a colored background behind the rest of the paragraph and set its width
```
p#para1 { background : cyan ; width : 70% }
```

4 Save the style sheet file alongside the HTML document then open the web page in a browser to see the elements styled by the ID selectors

Hot tip

If a class selector and an ID selector both attempt to style the same property of one element the ID selector value would be applied as it takes preference.

Selecting descendants

A descendant selector can be used in a style rule to select HTML elements by reference to an outer containing element from which they "descend". For example, a span element within a paragraph element descends from the paragraph element – so a descendant selector of **p span** could be used to select it for styling.

descendant.html

1. Create an HTML document containing an unordered list and an ordered list within a "div" container
```
<div id="menu">
<ul>
<li>Bigger Burger</li>
<li>Buffalo Wings</li>
<li>Deepcrust Pizza</li>
</ul>
<ol><li>Cola</li><li>Beer</li></ol>
</div>
```

descendant.css

2. Create a linked style sheet with style rules to color the items in each list
```
ul li { color : red }
ol li { color : blue }
```

3. Save the style sheet alongside the HTML document then open the web page in a browser to see the list items styled by descendant selectors

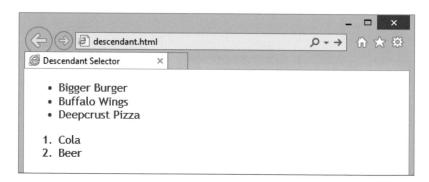

Although it is generally preferable to reference the element from which the target element directly descends it is sometimes useful to simply reference a higher level – say, that from which the containing element descends. This means that the direct containing element is omitted from the selector and the element is selected by reference to the higher level containing element.

4 Edit the style sheet by replacing the previous style rules with a single rule to color the items of both lists in a single color
#menu li { color : green }

5 Save the amended style sheet then refresh the browser window to see the list items styled without reference to their direct containing elements

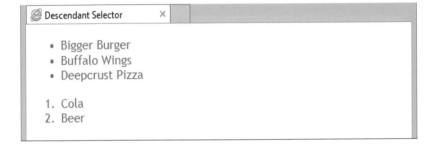

More specific selection can be made, however, by stating each containing element in the line of descent in a descendant selector.

6 Edit the style sheet once more by replacing the previous style rule with two style rules to color the items of both lists in a different colors
#menu ul li { color : orange }
#menu ol li { color : purple }

7 Save the newly-amended style sheet then refresh the browser window again to see the list items styled by reference to their lines of descent

Don't forget

In this case a descendant selector of **div li** would also select all list items but it is better to reference the **id** value so as not to select list items in other **div** elements.

27

Hot tip

State the line of descent wherever possible when using descendant selectors to make specific selections.

Selecting by relationship

Style rules can select elements for styling using the HTML document structure itself. The elements in all HTML documents are arranged in a hierarchical manner descending from the root **<html>** element. The next level contains the **<head>** and **<body>** elements. These each contain nested elements that may, in turn, contain further nested elements... and so on to complete the hierarchy. The hierarchy of a simple HTML document could resemble this tree view:

Hot tip

This tree view represents the HTML document in the example opposite.

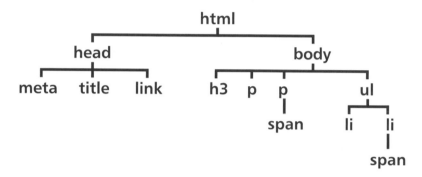

The hierarchy between a containing element and a nested element on the next hierarchical level can be described as a parent-child relationship. So **<html>** is the parent of the **<head>** and **<body>** elements, who are themselves children of the **<html>** element. Similarly, the **<head>** element is the parent of the **<meta>**, **<title>**, and **<link>** child elements, and the **<h3>**, **<p>**, and **<ul>** elements are all children of the **<body>** parent element.

Don't forget

As with people, all elements are a parent or a child, or in many cases they are both.

A style rule child selector can select specific child elements by stating the parent name followed by the **>** right angled-bracket character then the child name. For example, a child selector of **p > span** selects all span elements within paragraph elements.

The child selector can even state the hierarchy completely back to the root element if preferred, such as **html > body > p > span**.

Another selector that selects elements by relationship is the adjacent sibling selector. This selects the first sibling element after a specified element – by stating the specified element name followed by the **+** plus character then the sibling name. For example, an adjacent sibling selector of **h3 + p** selects any **<p>** paragraph element that immediately follows a **<h3>** heading element where both have the same parent.

1. Create an HTML document containing a heading, two paragraphs, a list, and including two spanned phrases

```
<body>
<h3>Heading : Child</h3>
<p>Paragraph : Child</p>
<p>Paragraph : Child
                <span>Span : Grandchild</span></p>
<ul>
<li>List Item : Grandchild</li>
<li>List Item : Grandchild
            <span>Span : Great Grandchild</span></li>
</ul>
</body>
```

relation.html

2. Create a linked style sheet with a style rule to select the first sibling immediately following the heading

```
h3 + p { background :  yellow }
```

relation.css

3. Next add a style rule to select the span child of the paragraph element

```
p > span { background : lime }
```

4. Now add style rules to select in turn each descendant element in the list by describing its hierarchy

```
body > ul { background : fuchsia }
body > ul > li { background : aqua }
body > ul > li > span { background : orange }
```

5. Save the style sheet alongside the HTML document then open the web page in a browser to see the elements styled by sibling and child selectors

Hot tip

The text in this example describes each element's relationship to the <body> element.

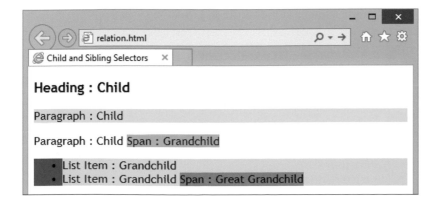

29

Selecting by attribute

Style rules can select HTML elements for styling by matching an attribute that the element contains. The selector in this case specifies the attribute name within square brackets. For example, a selector of *[src] would select all elements containing a **src** attribute – irrespective of their assigned values.

Additionally, the attribute selector can specify multiple attributes to select only those elements containing all the specified attributes. For example, a selector of *[src][alt] would select all elements containing both **src** and **alt** attributes – irrespective of their assigned values.

More specific selection is possible by stating an assigned value to match in the selector. For example, a selector of *[lang="en"] would select all elements containing a **lang** attribute that have an assigned value of **"en"**.

attribute.html

1 Create an HTML document with five anchor elements
<div><a id="top">Anchor</a></div> <hr>

<div><a href="http://www.google.com">Web Hyperlink</a></div> <hr>

<div><a href="http://www.google.com" title="Google"> Web Hyperlink + Title</a></div> <hr>

<div><a href="#top" title="Top of the Page" > Page Hyperlink</a></div> <hr>

<div><a id="bottom">Anchor</a></div>

attribute.css

2 Create a linked style sheet with a style rule to paint the background of all anchors containing an **id** attribute
a[id] { background : orange }

3 Add a style rule text to color the text in all hyperlinks containing an **href** attribute
a[href] { color : red }

4 Next add a style rule to paint the background of all hyperlinks containing both an **href** attribute and a **title** attribute
a[href][title] { background : yellow }

5 Now add a style rule to draw a border around all hyperlinks that have an href attribute assigned a #top value

a[href="#top"] { border : 0.2em solid blue }

6 Save the style sheet alongside the HTML document then open the web page in a browser to see styles applied to elements selected by their attributes

Don't forget

The * "wild card" universal selector selects all elements that match.

Selecting partial attributes

Style rules can select HTML elements for styling by matching partial attribute values. This allows the selector to target an element based upon the presence of any single word in an attribute containing a space-separated list of words. Typically, this technique might be used to match one of the words assigned to the **class** attribute of an HTML element.

The syntax to match a single word in an attribute list adds a ~ tilde character to the selector, such as ***[class~="word"]** – to match all elements that have a **class** attribute assigned a "word" value.

Additionally, a style rule selector can select an HTML element for styling by matching the beginning of an assigned attribute value. Typically, this technique might be used to match values assigned to HTML **lang** attribute values or a series of images.

The syntax to match the beginning of a value assigned to an HTML attribute adds a | pipe character to the selector, such as ***[lang|="es"]** – to match all elements that have a **lang** attribute assigned a value beginning with "es".

partial.html

1. Create an HTML document containing an ordered list in which all elements have a **class** attribute
```
<ol>
<li class="reptile">Alligator</li>
<li class="animal">Race Horse</li>
<li class="animal">Domestic Cat</li>
<li class="fish">Barracuda</li>
<li class="toy animal">Teddy Bear</li>
</ol>
```

2. Add an unordered list in which all elements have a **lang** attribute
```
<ul>
<li lang="en-us">Hello America</li>
<li lang="es">Hola Espa&ntilde;a</li>
<li lang="es-mx">Hola M&eacute;xico</li>
</ul>
```

3 Add a paragraph containing two sets of images

```
<p>
<img src="ring-1.png" alt="Ring Image">
        <img src="box-1.png" alt="Box Image">
<img src="ring-2.png" alt="Ring Image" >
        <img src="box-2.png" alt="Box Image" >
<img src="ring-3.png" alt="Ring Image" >
        <img src="box-3.png" alt="Box Image" >
</p>
```

Ring and box images – the red areas are transparent.

4 Save the HTML file, then create a style sheet with a rule to select elements in the ordered list according to the value assigned to their **class** attributes

```
*[class~="animal"] { background : lime }
```

partial.css

5 Now add a rule to select elements in the unordered list according to the beginning of the value assigned to their **lang** attributes

```
*[lang|="es"] { color : red ; background : yellow }
```

6 Next add rules to select **img** elements according to the beginning of the value assigned to their **src** attributes

```
*[src|="ring"] { background : fuchsia }
*[src|="box"] { background : aqua }
```

7 Save the style sheet alongside the HTML document then open the web page in a browser to see styles applied by selecting partial attribute values

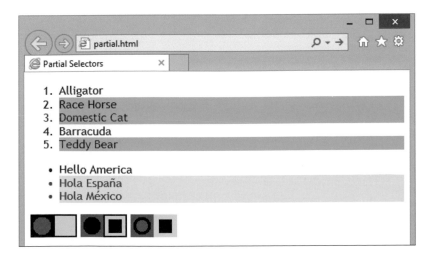

Evaluating importance

After the cascade considers the origin of style rules, as described on page 11, the browser then evaluates their "weight" to determine which rules have most weight and should, therefore, be applied.

Weight can be added to any style rule by including a CSS **!important** declaration to elevate its status. For example, the rule **h2 { color : red !important }** takes precedence over another rule of **h2 { color : blue }** and the red color will be applied.

Although regular Author style sheet rules take precedence over regular User and Browser style sheet rules, an **!important** User style sheet rule overrides an **!important** Author style sheet rule. So the cascade sorts style sheet rules by origin and weight into this order, from most weight to least weight:

(1) **!important** User style sheet rules

(2) **!important** Author style sheet rules

(3) regular Author style sheet rules

(4) regular User style sheet rules

(5) regular Browser style sheet rules

Where more than one style rule of equal weight targets properties of the same element the browser then evaluates their importance by examining their selector's "specificity" – to consider how specifically each one targets the element. The specificity evaluation process awards points for each selector component, which get stored in four "registers" for later comparison against the specificity value of conflicting selectors. So the specificity value can be expressed as a comma-separated list – in which 0,0,0,0 is a zero specificity value. The selector component points are awarded like this:

- For each element and pseudo-element in the selector add 0,0,0,1

- For each **class** attribute value, attribute selection, or pseudo-class in the selector add 0,0,1,0

- For each **id** attribute in the selector add 0,1,0,0

- For inline **style** attribute declarations add 1,0,0,0

In comparing specificity values the registers are examined individually, reading from left to right, until a difference is found. The style rule with the highest value in that register is then applied, For example, in comparing specificity values of 0,1,0,0 and 0,0,0,1 a difference occurs in the second register.

1 Create an HTML document containing three headings
```
<h2>Element style</h2>
<h2 id="heading-2">Identity style</h2>
<h2 class="headers">Class style</h2>
```

importance.html

2 Next create a linked style sheet containing rules that both target the heading elements' color property
```
h2 { color : yellow !important }
h2 { color : black }
```

importance.css

3 Now add rules that each target the heading elements' background property in different ways
```
h2 { background : aqua }              /* 0,0,0,1 */
body h2 { background : blue }         /* 0,0,0,2 */

#heading-2 { background : maroon }    /* 0,1,0,0 */
h2#heading-2 { background : red }     /* 0,1,0,1 */

h2.headers { background : olive }     /* 0,0,1,1 */
body h2.headers { background : green } /* 0,0,1,2 */
```

4 Save the style sheet alongside the HTML document then open the web page in a browser to see the elements styled after considering origin, weight, and specificity

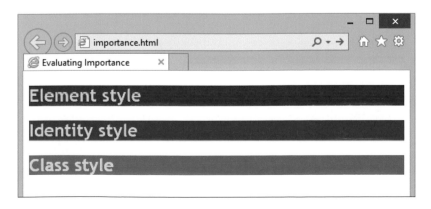

35

Summary

- A type selector selects all elements of the specified type and multiple elements can be specified as a comma-separated list

- The * universal selector can be used to select all elements

- The . class selector selects all elements containing a **class** attribute that has been assigned a specific value

- The # ID selector selects all elements containing an **id** attribute that has been assigned a specific value

- A descendant selector specifies both an element type and a type of element from which it descends, separated by space

- A > child selector specifies both the parent element type and the child element type from which it descends, to select the child elements

- The + adjacent sibling selector specifies an element type and the element type of an adjacent sibling to be selected

- The [] attribute selector specifies an element type followed by the name of an attribute within square brackets, to select all specified elements containing that attribute

- Optionally, a [] attribute selector can also specify an attribute value within the brackets to select only elements of the specified type that contain a specified attribute of that value

- An attribute selector can match a single word in an attribute list using the ~= syntax in the square brackets

- An attribute selector can match the beginning of an attribute value using the |= syntax in the square brackets

- A style rule can be made to override another by adding an **!important** declaration to elevate its status

- After the cascade arranges style rule importance by origin, it then considers their weight and specificity to determine which rules should be applied

3 Styling boxes

This chapter demonstrates how to style the boxes that contain web page content.

Recognizing content boxes

Content on a web page is displayed in a number of invisible rectangular boxes that are generated by the browser. These content boxes may be either "block level" or "inline".

Block-level content boxes normally have line breaks before and after the box, such as paragraph, heading and "div" elements.

Inline content boxes, on the other hand, do not add line breaks but are simply created within lines of text, such as span, emphasis, and hyperlink elements.

Each block-level content box comprises a core content area surrounded by optional areas for padding, border, and margins:

Style rules can specify values for the padding, border, and margin properties to control the appearance of content boxes. These all apply to block-level boxes but some properties, such as width and height, do not apply to inline boxes. Additionally, the margin and padding properties of inline boxes only apply to either side of the content – not the areas above and below the content.

When the padding, border, and margin properties all have a zero width the content box will be the same size as the content area, determined by the dimensions of the content.

Any padding, border, and margin areas that have a non-zero width are added outside the content area, so the content size remains the same but the box size increases.

The padding property extends the area around the content and inherits the background color of the content area. The border property extends the area around the content and any padding. The margin property extends the area around the content, any padding, and any border, with a transparent background.

Hot tip

Block-level content boxes are by default stacked on the page, one below another, whereas inline content boxes appear within a block-level box, one behind another.

1 Create an HTML document with four simple paragraphs, three with assigned **class** attribute values

```
<p>Content Box</p>
<p class="pad">Content Box - Padded</p>
<p class="pad bdr">Content Box - Padded + Border</p>
<p class="pad bdr mgn">Content Box -
                    Padded + Border + Margin</p>
```

box.html

2 Save the HTML document then create a linked style sheet with a style rule that sets the width and background color of the core content area

p { background : yellow ; width : 20em }

box.css

3 Next add a style rule to add some padding

p.pad { padding : 1em }

4 Now add a style rule to add a border

p.bdr { border : 0.5em red solid }

5 Finally add a style rule to add a margin

p.mgn { margin : 2em }

6 Save the style sheet alongside the HTML document then open the web page in a browser to see the content boxes with added padding, borders, and margin

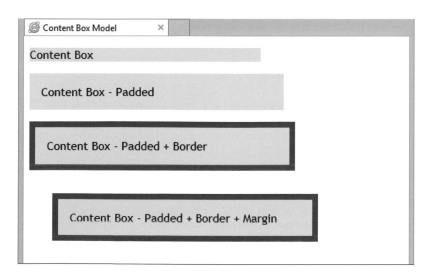

Changing display formats

A web page relies upon the creation of block-level content boxes, to determine its general layout, and the creation of inline content boxes within the blocks to determine its precise layout.

This places great emphasis on whether an element is considered block-level or inline to determine the display format. Generally the default display format for each element will be the most appropriate. For example, it's generally desirable to display list items on individual lines in a block-level list.

The display format of an element can also be explicitly determined by a style rule that assigns the **block** or **inline** keywords to that element's **display** property. This means that content can be displayed in a different format without changing the HTML tags. For example, list items can be displayed on a single line with a **display : inline** declaration.

Where two block-level elements follow each other the first can be made to be displayed as if it was an inline box within the beginning of the second block by assigning its **display** property the **run-in** keyword. For example, applying a run-in style rule to a heading that is followed by a paragraph will display the heading apparently within the start of the paragraph block.

Additionally an inline content-box can have its **display** property assigned an **inline-block** value to allow it to be displayed somewhat like a block-level content box. The inline-block still appears inline, as usual, but unlike regular inline content boxes its **width** and **height** properties can be assigned values to control its size.

display.html

1. Create an HTML document containing two unordered list blocks, with one assigned a **class** attribute value
```
<ul>
<li>Item 1 </li><li>Item 2 </li><li>Item 3 </li></ul>
<ul class="line">
<li>Item 1 </li><li>Item 2 </li><li>Item 3 </li></ul>
```

2. Next add two heading blocks, each followed by a paragraph block, with one assigned a **class** attribute value
```
<h2>Heading Block</h2><p>Paragraph Block</p>
<h2 class="run">Heading Block</h2>
<p>Paragraph Block</p>
```

3 Next add a paragraph block containing three inline hyperlink content boxes

```
<p>
<a href="1.html">Page 1</a>
<a href="2.html">Page 2</a>
<a href="3.html">Page 3</a>
</p>
```

4 Save the HTML document then create a linked style sheet with a rule to display one list's items inline

ul.line li { display : inline ; background : aqua }

display.css

5 Add another style rule to run one heading block into the following paragraph block

h2.run { display : run-in ; background : yellow }

6 Then add a style rule to change the inline hyperlink content boxes into inline blocks so their height and width can be adjusted

p a { display : inline-block ;
width : 4em ; height : 4em ; background : lime }

7 Save the style sheet alongside the HTML document then open the web page in a browser to see the content displayed in default and non-default display formats

Don't forget

Assigning a non-default display type to an element only changes the way it gets displayed – in the document tree inline elements are always descendants of block-level elements.

Sizing the content area

When assigning any non-zero value to a property the declaration must include a two-letter unit name to specify which unit of measurement to apply. The CSS specification provides the following unit names representing real world measurement:

Don't forget

Zero values can be assigned using just a "0" number – without specifying a unit name.

Unit :	Description :	Example :
in (inches)	American standard unit of length measurement	**div { width : 1in }**
cm (centimeters)	Metric unit of length where 2.54 centimeters is equivalent to 1 inch	**div { height : 2.54cm }**
mm (millimeters)	Metric unit of length (one tenth of one centimeter) where 25.4 millimeters is equivalent to 1 inch	**div { height : 25.4mm }**
pt (points)	Typographical unit of font height where 72 points is equivalent to 1 inch	**div { font-size : 72pt }**
pc (picas)	Typographical unit of font height where 6 picas is equivalent to 1 inch	**div { font-size : 6pc }**

The CSS specification also provides the following unit names representing relative values according to the viewing device:

Hot tip

A percentage value can also specify a relative size – where a value of 50% makes the target element half the size of its containing element.

Unit :	Description :	Example :
em (font size)	Abstract typographical unit of font size where 1em is equivalent to the height of a given font	**div { font-size : 14pt }** (1em = 14pt)
ex (font size)	Abstract typographical unit of font size where 1ex is equivalent to the height of lowercase "x" in a font (often 50% of 1em)	**div { font-size : 14pt }** (1ex = 7pt)
px (pixels)	Abstract unit representing the dots on a computer monitor where there are 1024 pixels on each line when the monitor resolution is 1024x768	**div { height : 100px };**

1 Create an HTML document containing 4 "div" elements
```
<div id="absolute">3in x &half;in</div>
<div id="container">400px x 200px
  <div id="percent">50% x 50%</div>
  <div id="relative">20em x 2em</div>
</div>
```

size.html

2 Save the HTML document then create a linked style sheet with a rule to size an element by absolute units
```
div#absolute { width : 3in ; height : 0.5in ;
                    background : red ; color : yellow }
```

size.css

3 Next add a rule to size an element by monitor resolution
```
div#container { width : 400px ; height : 200px ;
                    background : blue ; color : aqua }
```

4 Now add a rule to size an element by percentage
```
div#percent { width : 50% ; height : 50% ;
                    background : green ; color : yellow }
```

5 Then add a rule to size an element relative to font height
```
div#relative { width : 20em ; height : 2em ;
                    background : yellow ; color : blue }
```

6 Save the style sheet alongside the HTML document then open the web page in a browser to see the element sizes

Hot tip

It is often considered good practice to use **em** units wherever possible for maximum flexibility.

Controlling borders

Each content box can have a border comprising **border-width**, **border-color**, and **border-style** properties. A value can be specified to each of these individual properties to apply a uniform border to all four sides of the content box, or a space-separated list of values can be specified to apply different borders to each side:

- When two values are listed the first is applied to the top and bottom borders

- When three values are listed the first is applied to the top border, the second is applied to the left and right borders, and the third is applied to the bottom border

- When four values are listed they are applied clockwise to the top, right, bottom, and left borders

The default **border-width** value is **medium** (a computed value), and the default **border-color** value is inherited from the element's **color** property, but the default **border-style** is **none**. This means that the border will not be visible until a value is assigned – possible **border-style** values are **solid, double, dotted, dashed, groove, ridge, inset, outset, hidden,** and **none**.

Rather than creating separate style rules for the **border-width, border-color,** and **border-style** properties it is simpler to use the CSS shorthand technique that specifies a value for each of these three properties to a **border** property as a space-separated list. This uniformly styles each side of the content box with a border of the specified width, color, and style. For example, a style rule declaration of **border : 0.5in red dotted** would apply a half-inch wide red dotted border to all four sides of the content box.

If it is desirable to have different styles, the borders on each side of a content box can be individually styled by creating rules for the element's **border-top, border-right, border-bottom,** and **border-left** properties. The CSS shorthand technique can also be used with these properties to specify a width, color, and style for the individual side as a space-separated list. For example, a style rule declaration of **border-bottom : 0.5in red dotted** would apply a half-inch wide red dotted border to just the bottom side of the content box.

Hot tip

The **outset** border style can be used to create the appearance of a raised button – and the **inset** border style can be used to create the appearance of a depressed button.

1 Create an HTML document containing four paragraphs
```
<p id="p1">Solid - Inherit - Medium</p>
<p id="p2">Top: Dotted - Orange - 0.2em
            <br>Bottom: Dashed - Green - 0.2em</p>
<p id="p3">Ridge Double - Blue - 1em</p>
<p id="p4">Outset - Yellow - 1em</p>
```

border.html

2 Save the HTML document then create a linked style sheet with a rule to add a border that inherits a color
```
#p1 { color : red ; border : solid }
```

border.css

3 Next add a rule with shorthand declarations to create a border above and below the content area only
```
#p2 { border-top : 0.5em orange dotted ;
      border-bottom : 0.5em green dashed }
```

4 Now add a rule creating a border from separate properties
```
#p3 { border-style : ridge double ;
      border-width : 1em ;
      border-color : blue }
```

5 Then add a rule creating a border on all four sides using the recommended CSS shorthand technique
```
#p4 { border : 1em yellow outset }
```

6 Save the style sheet alongside the HTML document then open the web page in a browser to see the borders

Adding padding

Each content box can have "padding" space added around the core content area by a style rule assigning a value to the **padding** property. A single value can be specified to apply a uniform padding width to all four sides of the content area, or a space-separated list of values can be specified to apply different padding widths to each side:

- When two values are listed the first is applied to the top and bottom sides and the second is applied to the left and right

- When three values are listed the first is applied to the top side, the second is applied to the left and right sides, and the third is applied to the bottom side

- When four values are listed they are applied clockwise to the top, right, bottom, and left sides

The padding area surrounds the core content area and extends to the outer edges of the border area if a border is specified – right up to the beginning of the margin area. The element's background fills the core content area and the padding area, so that any specified background color gets automatically applied to both the core content area and the padding area.

The **padding** property can be specified as a unit value or as a percentage value. When a percentage is specified the padding width is calculated using the width and height of the containing element and the padding area size will be adjusted if the size of the containing element gets changed.

Typically a padding area is specified when adding a border to an element to increase the space between the content and the border.

If it is desirable to have different padding widths on each side of a content box the padding can be individually styled by creating rules for the element's **padding-top, padding-right, padding-bottom**, and **padding-left** properties. For example, style rule declarations of **padding-top : 0.5in ; padding-bottom : 0.5in** would apply a half-inch padding area to top and bottom sides. Alternatively, the same result can be achieved using the CSS shorthand with a declaration of **padding : 0.5in 0 0.5in 0**.

1 Create an HTML document containing three paragraphs that each include a span element and are separated by horizontal ruled lines

```
<p>Horizontally
        <span id="pad-h">Padded</span> Content.</p>
<hr>
<p>Vertically
        <span id="pad-v">Padded</span> Content.</p>
<hr>
<p>Horizontally and Vertically
        <span id="pad-hv">Padded</span> Content.</p>
```

padding.html

2 Save the HTML document then create a linked style sheet with rules to color the paragraph and span elements

```
p { background : aqua }
span { background : yellow ; border : 0.3em red dashed }
```

padding.css

3 Next add a style rule to add padding to the left and right sides of the first span content box

```
span#pad-h { padding : 0 3em 0 3em }
```

4 Now add a style rule to add padding to the top and bottom sides of the second span content box

```
span#pad-v { padding : 1em 0 1em 0 }
```

5 Then add a style rule to add uniform padding to all sides of the third span element

```
span#pad-hv { padding : 1em }
```

6 Save the style sheet alongside the HTML file then open the web page in a browser to see the added padding

Don't forget

Notice how the background color fills the content area and padding area – extending up to the outer edge of the border area.

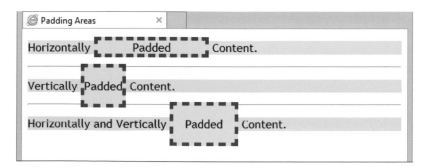

Setting margins

Each content box can have outer "margin" space added around the entire content, padding, and border areas by a style rule assigning a value to the **margin** property. A single value can be specified to apply a uniform margin width to all four sides of the content box, or a space-separated list of values can be specified to apply different margin widths to each side:

- When two values are listed the first is applied to the top and bottom sides and the second is applied to the left and right

- When three values are listed the first is applied to the top side, the second is applied to the left and right sides, and the third is applied to the bottom side

- When four values are listed they are applied clockwise to the top, right, bottom, and left sides

The **margin** property has a default value of zero but in reality the browser applies its own intrinsic default values to allow spacing between elements. For example, heading elements always allow a margin area before a following paragraph element.

The **margin** property can be specified as a unit value, or as a percentage value, or with the **auto** keyword to have the browser compute a suitable margin.

Margins do not inherit any background and are always transparent – they merely separate elements by a specified distance.

If it is desirable to have different margin widths on each side of a content box the margin can be individually styled by creating rules for the element's **margin-top, margin-right, margin-bottom,** and **margin-left** properties. For example, style rule declarations of **margin-top : 0.5in ; margin-bottom : 0.5in** would apply a half-inch margin area to top and bottom sides. Alternatively, the same result can be achieved using the CSS shorthand with a declaration of **margin : 0.5in 0 0.5in 0**.

Hot tip

The ability to automatically compute the margin size is essential for centering content – as described on page 58.

Hot tip

The margin width for each side can be set using the CSS **margin** shorthand by setting sides requiring no margin to zero – always use the shorthand.

① Create an HTML document containing three "div" elements that each contain a heading element and a paragraph element

```
<div><h2>Heading - Default Margin</h2>
<p>Paragraph - Default Margin</p></div>
<div><h2 class="zero">Heading - No Margin</h2>
<p class="zero">Paragraph - No Margin</p></div>
<div><h2 class="left">Heading - Left Margin</h2>
<p class="left">Paragraph - Left Margin</p></div>
```

margin.html

② Save the HTML document then create a linked style sheet with rules to color the elements

```
div { border : 1px solid black }
h2 { background : lime }
p { background : orange }
```

margin.css

③ Next add a style rule to remove all margins from the second heading and paragraph element content boxes

```
.zero { margin : 0 }
```

④ Now add a style rule to add a left margin only to the third heading and paragraph element content boxes

```
.left { margin : 0 0 0 0.5in }
```

⑤ Save the style sheet alongside the HTML file then open the web page in a browser to see the margin styles

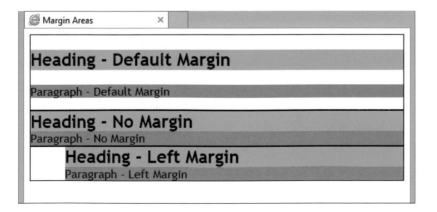

Painting colors

The listed examples so far in this book have employed color keywords to represent the 17 CSS "standard" colors as below:

Red		Green		Blue
Fuchsia		Lime		Aqua
Maroon		Olive		Navy
Orange	Yellow		White	Purple
Silver	Black		Teal	Gray

While the standard named colors are convenient to use they provide only a limited choice. Fortunately CSS allows authors to create their own custom colors.

Each color can be defined by the amount of red, green, and blue that needs to be mixed together to form that particular color. For example, the standard olive color comprises 50% red, 50% green and 0% blue. This can be expressed in RGB notation form as **rgb(50%, 50%, 0%)** for assignment to a CSS property like this:

h1 { color : rgb(50%, 50%, 0%) }   /* Olive headings */

Specifying different amounts of red, green, and blue, in this way the author can assign to a property any custom color desired.

As an alternative to specifying each color component as a percentage the author may choose an integer value in the range 0-255 for each component. In this format the RGB notation for the standard olive color looks like this:

h1 { color : rgb(128, 128, 0) }   /* Olive headings */

A second alternative to specifying each color component as a percentage allows the author to choose a hexadecimal value in the range 00-FF for each component. In this format the assignment for the standard olive color looks like this:

h1 { color : #808000 }   /* Olive headings */

The table opposite lists the ways in which each standard color can be assigned to a property using these various methods.

Don't forget

Web browsers often recognize many more color names (often up to 140) but those shown here are the standard color names defined in the CSS specifications.

Color :	Percentage :	Integer :	Hex :
Black	rgb(0%,0%,0%)	rgb(0,0,0)	#000000
Red	rgb(100%,0%,0%)	rgb(255,0,0)	#FF0000
Orange	rgb(100%,65%,0%)	rgb(255,165,0)	#FFA500
Yellow	rgb(100%,100%,0%)	rgb(255,255,0)	#FFFF00
Fuchsia	rgb(100%,0%,100%)	rgb(255,0,255)	#FF00FF
Lime	rgb(0%,100%,0%)	rgb(0,255,0)	#00FF00
Aqua	rgb(0%,100%,100%)	rgb(0,255,255)	#00FFFF
Blue	rgb(0%,0%,100%)	rgb(0,0,255)	#0000FF
White	rgb(100%,100%,100%)	rgb(255,255,255)	#FFFFFF
Maroon	rgb(50%,0%,0%)	rgb(128,0,0)	#800000
Olive	rgb(50%,50%,0%)	rgb(128,128,0)	#808000
Purple	rgb(50%,0%,50%)	rgb(128,0,128)	#800080
Green	rgb(0%,50%,0%)	rgb(0,128,0)	#008000
Teal	rgb(0%,50%,50%)	rgb(0,128,128)	#008080
Navy	rgb(0%,0%,50%)	rgb(0,0,128)	#000080
Gray	rgb(50%,50%,50%)	rgb(128,128,128)	#808080
Silver	rgb(75%,75%,75%)	rgb(192,192,192)	#C0C0C0

Hexadecimal color values comprising three pairs of matching digits can alternatively be expressed using CSS shorthand notation that represents each pair of digits as a single digit. For example, the hexadecimal value for the standard red color is **#FF0000** but can be specified in shorthand as **#F00**. Similarly black **#000000** can be written as **#000** and white **#FFFFFF** as **#FFF**.

The author is free to choose which color notation method to use according to their preference. Declarations in the style rules below show how each method might be used to specify a custom color:

```
h1 { color : rgb( 85%, 15%, 0% ) }        /* A custom red */
h2 { color : rgb( 0, 192, 12 ) }          /* A custom green */
h3 { color : #042BDF }                    /* A custom blue */
h4 { color : #DE2 }        /* A custom yellow (#DDEE22) */
```

Hot tip

In hex notation, you can specify "web safe" consistent colors by using only digits that are multiples of 3 for the red, green and blue.

Repeating backgrounds

Each content box can have a background color specified by assigning a valid color value to its **background** property. Alternatively an image can be specified for the background by assigning a **url(*filename*)** value, where *filename* is the path to an image file – this should not be enclosed within quotes.

The **background-color** and **background-image** properties can be used to specify both a background color and a background image. Any specified background image will normally be positioned at the top left corner of the content box. The default behavior of the browser's **background-repeat** property is set to **repeat** so the image will be tiled, row-by-row, across the content box.

Hot tip

Use the **background** property shorthand rather than the various individual properties – to keep the style sheet more concise.

The tiling behavior can be modified by assigning different values to the **background-repeat** property where values of **repeat-x** restricts the tiling pattern to one horizontal row and **repeat-y** restricts the tiling pattern to one vertical column. Tiling can also be prevented by assigning a **no-repeat** value so that a single copy of the image appears at the top left corner of the content box.

Background images are placed on a layer above the background's color layer so specifying an image with transparent areas will allow the background color to shine through.

Using CSS shorthand the color, image, and repeat values can simply be assigned as a space-separated list to the **background** property. These may appear in any order and default values are assumed for any value not specified in the list. For example, the **background-repeat** property is assumed to have a **repeat** value unless another value is specified.

HTML

background.html

1 Create an HTML document with four paragraphs that each contain a span element
<p><span>Repeat - Default</span></p>

<p id="x"><span>Repeat-X</span></p>

<p id="y"><span>Repeat-Y</span></p>

<p id="no"><span>No Repeat</span></p>

2 Save the HTML document then create a linked style sheet containing a rule to style the span elements
span { background : yellow ; margin : 0 0 0 10em }

3 Next add a style rule to specify the background color, background image, and height of each paragraph
p { background : url(tile.png) fuchsia repeat ;
**   height : 3.5em }**

4 Now add a style rule to modify the tiling behavior of the second paragraph to one row
p#x { background-repeat : repeat-x }

5 Then add a style rule to modify the tiling behavior of the third paragraph to one column
p#y { background-repeat : repeat-y }

6 Finally add a style rule to modify the tiling behavior of the fourth paragraph to just one copy of the image
p#no { background-repeat : no-repeat }

7 Save the style sheet alongside the HTML document then open the web page in a browser to see the background color and image applied

background.css

tile.png – the red areas are transparent.

Don't forget

The **repeat** value could be omitted from the rule in step 3 – as that is the default value.

53

Positioning backgrounds

A background image is, by default, positioned at the top left corner of the content box but this can be modified by specifying a different value to the **background-position** property. This can accept keywords of either **left, center, right, top,** and **bottom.** Two of these keywords may be used to specify the position, separated by a space, such as **top center.** Alternatively just one of these keywords can be specified and the second value will be assumed to be **center.**

The **background-position** property can also be assigned percentage values to specify the position with greater precision, taken from the dimensions of the containing element. The keywords have the equivalent to these percentages:

X-Axis :			Y-Axis :	
				top (0%)
left (0%)	center (50%)	right (100%)		center (50%)
				bottom (100%)

When specifying position with percentages the first value sets the X-axis position and the second value sets the Y-axis position. If only one percentage is specified the second is assumed to be 50%. Interestingly, when computing the background image position the browser first identifies a point within the image at the specified coordinates, then places that point at the same coordinates within the content box. For example, with values of **50% 50%** the browser first identifies a point at the exact center of the image then places that point at the exact center of the content box.

The **background-attachment** property has a **scroll** value by default so the background image scrolls with the page but a style rule can specify a **fixed** value so it remains at specified coordinates relative to the viewport when the page gets scrolled.

Both **background-position** and **background-attachment** property values can be specified to the CSS **background** property, along with the **background-color, background-image,** and **background-repeat** values described on the previous page.

Hot tip

The **background-position** property can also accept unit values to specify an offset position of the top left corner of the image from the top left corner of the content box. But this is only useful where the size of the content box cannot change – use keywords or percentages for greater flexibility.

1 Create an HTML document with three paragraphs that each contain a span element
```
<p><span>Top Left - Default</span></p>
<p id="p1"><span>Bottom Left</span></p>
<p id="p2"><span>20% 50%</span></p>
```

position.html

2 Save the HTML document then create a linked style sheet containing rules to style the spans and paragraphs
```
span { background : yellow ; margin : 0 0 0 10em }
p { background : url(tile.png) fuchsia no-repeat ;
                                        height : 3.5em }
```

position.css

3 Now add rules to position paragraph background images using keywords and percentages
```
p#p1 { background-position : bottom left }
p#p2 { background-position : 20% 50% }
```

4 Finally add a rule to fix a background image in the page that will remain positioned when the page gets scrolled
```
body { background : url(tile.png) no-repeat
                                bottom right fixed }
```

5 Save the style sheet alongside the HTML document then open the web page in a browser to see the positioned background images

Summary

- Block-level content boxes add line breaks before and after the box – but inline content boxes appear within lines of text

- The core content area of a content box can be surrounded by **padding, border,** and **margin** areas

- A content box's **display** property can be used to change its display format from block-level to inline, and vice versa

- Content box dimensions can be specified to **width** and **height** properties as absolute values of **in, cm, mm, pt,** and **pc** units, or as relative values of **em, ex,** and **px** measurements

- The **border** property can specify the individual **border-width, border-color,** and **border-style** properties using CSS shorthand

- Border styles may be **solid, double, dotted, dashed, groove, ridge, inset, outset, hidden** or **none**

- The **padding** property can specify the individual **padding-top, padding-right, padding-bottom,** and **padding-left** properties using CSS shorthand

- The **margin** property can specify the individual **margin-top, margin-right, margin-bottom,** and **margin-left** properties using CSS shorthand

- Colors can be specified using the standard color keywords, or as a three-part **rgb()** value with percentage or numerical parts, or as a single hexadecimal value

- The **background** property can specify the individual **background-color, background-image, background-repeat, background-position,** and **background-attachment** properties using CSS shorthand

- Background images can be specified as a **url()** value in which the path to the image file is stated within the parentheses

4 Controlling layout

This chapter demonstrates how to position content boxes to control page layout.

Centering content boxes

One of the basic requirements in displaying document components is the ability to horizontally center blocks of content – in the same way provided by the old HTML **<center>** tag.

In CSS the ability to horizontally center block-level elements is provided by the **margin** property and the **auto** keyword.

When the **auto** keyword is specified to an element's **margin** property the browser first calculates the distance to the left and right of that element, up to the boundaries of its containing element, then divides the total in half to compute the value of each side margin. For example, applying a **margin : auto** to a "div" element of 80px width, that is contained within an outer element of 200px width, the browser divides the total difference of 120px in half then applies 60px wide margins to each side of the div element – so it gets positioned centrally within the containing element.

Notice that **margin : auto** does not center vertically but merely sets the top and bottom margins to zero, so there are no margin areas above or below the element block.

It is important to recognize that **margin : auto** centers block-level content boxes and should not be confused with **text-align : center** that can be used to center content within inline content boxes.

Beware

Assigning an **auto** value to the **margin** property removes top and bottom margins – just as if they had been assigned a zero value.

center.html

1 Create an HTML document with a "div" element containing two further elements
<div>Default Position
  <div class="inner">Default Position</div>
  <div class="inner center">Centered Block</div>
</div>

2 Now add another "div" element containing three further elements
<div class="center">Centered Block
<div class="inner">Default Position</div>
<div class="center inner">Centered Block</div>
<div class="center inner center-text">
            Centered Block + Centered Content</div>
</div>

3 Save the HTML document then create a linked style sheet containing a style rule to specify default width, margin, and colors for each element
div { width : 20em ; margin : 0 0 2em 0 ;
border : 0.1em solid black ; background : orange }

center.css

4 Next add a style rule over-writing the previous rule for inner elements
div.inner { margin : 0 ; width : 10em ; background : yellow }

5 Now add a rule to center inner elements
div.center { margin : auto ; background : aqua }

6 Finally add a style rule to center content within an inner element
div.center-text { text-align : center ; background : lime }

7 Save the style sheet alongside the HTML document then open the web page in a browser to see the centered content boxes and centered content

59

Hot tip

When the browser window gets resized the second outer "div" element automatically gets repositioned to become horizontally centered again.

Positioning boxes absolutely

When laying out the element content boxes of a web page the CSS **position** property has a default value of **static** – representing the normal flow positioning scheme. Assigning a different value to an element's **position** property allows that element to be removed from the normal flow so it can be positioned independently.

Alternatives to the default **static** value can be specified using the **absolute**, **relative**, and **fixed** keywords to specify an alternative positioning scheme to that of the normal flow layout.

The **absolute**, **relative**, and **fixed** positioning schemes each use one or more of the CSS "offset" properties **top**, **right**, **bottom**, and **left**, to define their position.

When the position property is specified as **absolute** the positioning scheme places the element at the specified offset distance from the boundaries of its containing element. For example, a "div" element with top and left values of 100px will be positioned 100px below and to the right of its container boundaries.

Don't forget

Each outer content box remains at its absolute position to the window when the browser window gets resized.

absolute.html

1 Create an HTML document with four "div" elements that each contain an inner div element
```
<div class="top-left large">Top:0 Left:0
 <div class="btm-right small">Bottom:0 Right:0</div>
</div>

<div class="top-right large">Top:0 Right:0
 <div class="btm-left small">Bottom:0 Left:0</div>
</div>

<div class="btm-left large">
                        <br><br><br>Bottom:0 Left:0
 <div class="top-right small">Top:0 Right:0</div>
</div>

<div class="btm-right large">
                        <br><br><br>Bottom:0 Right:0
 <div class="top-left small">Top:0 Left:0</div>
</div>
```

2 Save the HTML document then create a linked style sheet with rules to set the absolute size of the elements
div.large { width : 200px ; height : 90px ;
                                         border : 1px solid black }
div.small { width : 80px ; height : 50px ;
                                         border : 1px solid black }

absolute.css

3 Now add style rules to set the absolute position of each element
div.top-left { position : absolute ; top : 0px ; left : 0px ;
                                         background : lime }

div.top-right { position : absolute ; top : 0px ; right : 0px ;
                                         background : aqua }

div.btm-left { position : absolute ;
               bottom : 0px ; left : 0px ; background : yellow }

div.btm-right { position : absolute ;
               bottom : 0px ; right : 0px ; background : orange }

4 Save the style sheet alongside the HTML document then open the web page in a browser to see the content boxes positioned at absolute coordinates

Stacking content boxes

Changing from the **static** default positioning scheme, by assigning the **absolute** value to the **position** property, allows elements to overlap – stacking one above the other in the same order they are listed in the HTML code.

The stacking order can be explicitly specified, however, in CSS by assigning an integer value to the **z-index** property of each element. The element with the highest value appears uppermost, then beneath that appears the element with the next highest value, and so on.

So the **absolute** positioning scheme allows the element position to be precisely controlled in three dimensions using XYZ coordinates – along the X axis with the **left** and **right** offset properties, along the Y axis using the **top** and **bottom** offset properties, and along the Z axis using the **z-index** stacking order property.

stack.html

1 Create an HTML document containing four "div" elements to be positioned overlapping

<div id="pale-gray"> </div>

<div id="lite-gray"> </div>

<div id="dark-gray"> </div>

<div id="text-box">Text content here on the top of the element stack - lower offset elements create a drop shadow effect</div>

2 Save the HTML document then create a linked style sheet containing a rule to set the size of all elements
div { width : 400px ; height : 50px }

stack.css

3 Next add a style rule to position the uppermost element
div#text-box {   position : absolute ;
top : 20px ; left : 20px ;
background : yellow ; z-index : 4 }

4 Now add a rule to position the next element below
div#dark-gray { position : absolute ;
top : 24px ; left : 24px ;
background : #666 ; z-index : 3 }

5 Then add a rule to position an element further below
div#lite-gray {   position : absolute ;
top : 28px ; left : 28px ;
background : #999 ; z-index : 2 }

6 Finally add a rule to position the lowest element
div#pale-gray { position : absolute ;
top : 32px ; left : 32px ;
background : #CCC ; z-index : 1 }

7 Save the style sheet alongside the HTML document then open the web page in a browser to see the elements positioned in all three dimensions

Hot tip

A smaller offset creates a more convincing drop shadow effect – a large offset is used here to illustrate the contribution of each element.

Positioning boxes relatively

In contrast to the **absolute** positioning scheme, which entirely removes an element from the normal flow layout, a **relative** positioning scheme adjusts the position of an element relative to the position it would originally occupy in the normal flow layout.

Changing from the default **static** positioning scheme, by assigning the **relative** value to the CSS **position** property, allows elements to be repositioned from their normal flow layout position using the offset properties **top**, **right**, **bottom** and **left**.

For example, specifying a **top** value of -18px moves the selected element up and specifying a **left** value of 100px moves it to the right – but crucially the space occupied by its original layout position is preserved. Applying these relative position values to a span element within a paragraph has this effect:

a repositioned span element

There is   on this line - it pays no heed to other paragraph content for it is an inline content box

Notice how the original content is shifted from its normal flow layout position into a newly-created content box positioned at the specified distance relative to its original position. This relative position will be maintained, even when the position of the outer containing element is changed.

So while **absolute** positioning may typically control the position of the outer element the **relative** positioning scheme is often useful to control the position of nested inner elements.

relative.html

1. Create an HTML document containing four nested "div" elements to be positioned overlapping

```
<div id="pale-gray">
 <div id="lite-gray">
  <div id="dark-gray">
   <div id="text-box">Text content here on the innermost
       element - outer offset elements create a drop
       shadow effect</div>
  </div>
 </div>
</div>
```

2 Save the HTML document then create a linked style sheet containing a rule to set the size and color of the outermost containing element
div#pale-gray { width : 400px ; height : 50px ;
                        background : #CCC ; margin : 20px }

relative.css

3 Next add a style rule to position the first nested element relative to the outermost containing element
div#lite-gray { position : relative ; left : -4px ; top : -4px ;
                        height : 100% ; background : #999 }

4 Now add a style rule to position the second nested element relative to the first nested element
div#dark-gray { position : relative ; left : -4px ; top : -4px ;
                        height : 100% ; background : #666 }

5 Finally add a style rule to position the innermost nested element relative to the second nested element
div#text-box { position : relative ; left : -4px ; top : -4px ;
                        height : 100% ; background : lime }

6 Save the style sheet alongside the HTML document then open the web page in a browser to see the nested elements positioned relative to their containing elements

Hot tip

The **margin** property is only set on the outer element simply to move the content away from the edge of the window.

Fixing constant positions

A **fixed** positioning scheme, like the **absolute** positioning scheme, completely removes the selected element's content box from the normal flow layout. But unlike **absolute** positioning, where offset values relate to the boundaries of the containing element, in **fixed** positioning the offset values relate to the viewport – the position is relative to the browser window, not to any part of the document.

Usefully, element positions can be fixed to emulate a frame-style interface where some frames remain at a constant position regardless of how the regular page is scrolled. For example, a banner header frame can be fixed at the top of the page so it remains constantly visible even when the page is scrolled.

fixed.html

1   Create an HTML document containing a heading element and a paragraph with a tall image to scroll
```
<h1>Header</h1>
<p>
<img src="ruler.png" width="71" height="521" alt="Ruler">
</p>
```

fixed.css

2   Save the HTML document then create a linked style sheet with a rule to fix the heading element to the top of the browser window and above other page content
```
h1 { position : fixed ; top : 0 ; left : 0 ; margin : 0 ;
            background : lime ; width : 100% ; z-index : 2 }
```

3   Now add a style rule to position the paragraph below the heading element
```
p { position : absolute ; top : 100px ; z-index : 1 }
```

4   Save the style sheet alongside the HTML document then open the web page in a browser to see the elements positioned by the style rules

5   Now scroll the browser window to see the heading remain in place while the paragraph content slides beneath it

ruler.png

Hot tip

Fixed positioning is sometimes used to display an identity logo that remains visible at a constant position regardless of where the page is scrolled.

Floating content boxes

The CSS **float** property allows a content box to be positioned at the side boundary of its containing element – using the **left** or **right** keywords to specify the preferred side. Typically this feature is used to flow text around images that have been floated to the side of a containing paragraph element.

You can also explicitly prevent text flowing alongside a floated content box using the CSS **clear** property – specifying **left, right,** or **both** keywords to determine which side must be clear, so that text will begin below the floated content box.

float.html

1. Create an HTML document containing three paragraphs and two images
```
<p>Massive acceleration - the forbidden fruit! It's easy to avoid such unlawful <img src="viper-1.png" width="150" height="128" alt="Viper Front"> activities in a normal vehicle. But there is an evil serpent; a Viper that tempts you to take a bite out of the asphalt. With a tasty 500-hp V10 powering a mere 3,300-lb roadster, the Dodge Viper SRT-10 tricks you into playing music with the loud pedal.</p>

<p>This car is too excessive, too epic for most people to use on a daily basis. <img src="viper-2.png" width="155" height="115" alt="Viper Rear">But for otherwise nice couples who need only two seats this is the car that will shame those who come up against them.</p>

<p class="clear">If you can afford to... Buy one. You'll like it.</p>
```

float.css

2. Save the HTML document then create a linked style sheet with a rule to color all paragraph backgrounds
```
p { background : yellow }
```

3. Now add a style rule to float the first image to the right side of its containing paragraph element and add a border
```
img[src="viper-1.png"] { float : right ;
                         border : 3px dashed red }
```

4. Next add a style rule to float the second image to the left side of its containing paragraph element and add a border
```
img[src="viper-2.png"] { float : left ;
                         border : 3px dashed blue }
```

5 Save the style sheet alongside the HTML document then open the web page in a browser to see the floated images

6 Edit the style sheet to add a rule that prevents the final paragraph flowing alongside the second floated image
p.clear { clear : left }

7 Save the style sheet once more then refresh the browser window to see the final paragraph now appear below the second image

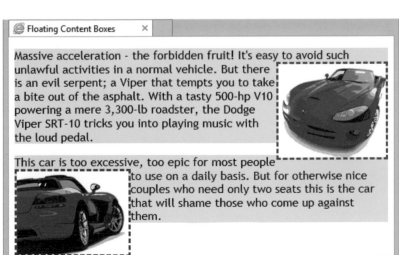

Clipping & handling overflow

Although CSS provides many controls to specify the precise size and position of content boxes there is no guarantee that their content will fit neatly within their boundaries in all circumstances. For example, consider the effect of increasing the font size of text content that fits snugly within a block-level content box – the text will then "overflow" outside the box boundaries.

Overflowing content is generally **visible** by default, but the CSS **overflow** property can specify alternative handling behaviors using the **hidden** or **scroll** keywords.

Conversely, the content within absolutely-positioned block-level content boxes can be cropped using the **clip** property – the rectangular section to remain visible being identified by the coordinates of its corner points. In CSS these coordinates are assigned to the **clip** property as a comma-separated list within the parentheses of the special **rect()** keyword, always in the order of top-left, top-right, bottom-right, bottom-left.

overflow.html

patch.png

1. Create an HTML document with six "div" elements that each contain the same image
```
<div class = "crop auto-clip">
        <img src = "patch.png" alt="Blocks"></div>

<div class = "crop blok-clip">
        <img src = "patch.png" alt="Blocks" ></div>

<div class = "crop line-clip">
        <img src = "patch.png" alt="Blocks" ></div>

<div class = "spill show-overflow">
        <img src = "patch.png" alt="Blocks" ></div>

<div class = "spill hide-overflow">
        <img src = "patch.png" alt="Blocks" ></div>

<div class = "spill keep-overflow">
        <img src = "patch.png" alt="Blocks" ></div>
```

overflow.css

2. Save the HTML document then create a linked style sheet with rules that specify the absolute position and size of each div element
```
div.crop{ position : absolute ; top : 20px ;
                        width : 100px ; height : 100px }
div.spill { position : absolute ; top : 150px ;
                        width : 75px ; height : 75px }
```

3 Add a style rule that allows the first image to be automatically cropped to the full image size
div.auto-clip { left : 20px ; clip : auto }

4 Next add style rules that crop the visible part of the second and third image to reveal only those parts of the image within specified coordinates
div.blok-clip
{ left : 140px ; clip : rect(25px, 100px, 100px, 25px) }

div.line-clip
{ left : 260px ; clip : rect(25px, 100px, 50px, 0px) }

5 Now add a style rule that allows those parts of the fourth image that overflow the content box to be visible
div.show-overflow { left : 20px ; overflow : visible }

6 Add a style rule to hide those parts of the fifth image that overflow the content box
div.hide-overflow { left : 140px ; overflow : hidden }

7 Finally add a style rule to hide those parts of the sixth image that overflow the content box and provide scroll bars so hidden parts can be viewed
div.keep-overflow { left : 260px ; overflow : scroll }

8 Save the style sheet alongside the HTML document then open the web page in a browser to see the cropped images and compare how the overflow is handled

Hot tip

The ability to toggle content visibility, between visible and hidden, presents exciting dynamic possibilities – see chapter 7 for more details and examples.

71

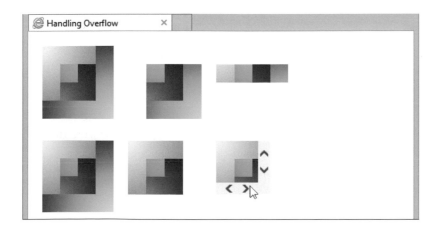

Constructing columns

Traditionally, web page authors have used HTML tables to control how page content is laid out by creating a borderless grid of cells into which components of the page are placed. This method works well enough for general layout but lacks the precise control offered by CSS. For example, the **absolute** positioning scheme allows components to be positioned easily with pinpoint accuracy but this could not be achieved easily using tables. Thus CSS provides a superior layout method so web page authors are now discouraged from using HTML tables for this purpose.

Moving to page layout with CSS invariably raises questions of how best to control the page content. The following example suggests one way to create a common page layout featuring a header and footer plus three content columns.

columns.html

tile.png – the red areas are transparent.

1 Create an HTML document containing "div" elements for header and content panels, all wrapped in an outer container element that is followed by a footer element
<div id="wrapper">

**<div id="hdr">Header Panel
**
<img src="tile.png" width="250" height="25" alt="Box">
</div>

<div id="nav">Navigation Panel
<ul><li>Link<li>Link</ul></div>

**<div id="ads">Supplement Panel
**
<img src="tile.png" width="75" height="100" alt="Box">
</div>

**<div id="txt">Content Panel
**
<img src="tile.png" width="150" height="200" alt="Box">
</div>

</div> <div id="ftr">Footer Panel</div>

columns.css

2 Save the HTML document then create a linked style sheet with a rule to remove all margins and padding, and to center all content
* { margin : 0 ; padding : 0 ; text-align : center }

3 Add a rule to ensure the page is the entire window height
html, body { height : 100% }

4 Now add a rule to have the container element use the entire window area – except for a bottom margin area where the footer will appear
#wrapper { min-height : 100% ; height : auto !important ; height : 100% ; margin : 0 auto -30px }

5 Next add style rules to set the header and footer heights and background color
#hdr { height : 60px ; background : aqua }
#ftr { height : 30px ; background : aqua }

6 Finally add rules to position and color the three columns
#nav { float : left ; width : 100px ; background : yellow }
#ads { float : right ; width : 100px ; background : fuchsia }
#txt { margin : 0 100px ; background : lime }

7 Save the style sheet alongside the HTML document then open the web page in a browser to see the page layout

Hot tip

This example solves the issue of how to create a "sticky footer" that always remains at the bottom of the window.

Don't forget

An image is included in this example, stretched to various dimensions, just to represent simple page content.

Summary

- A **margin : auto** rule horizontally centers block-level content boxes, acting much like the old HTML **<center>** tag

- A **text-align : center** rule horizontally centers text within a content box

- The **absolute, relative,** and **fixed** positioning schemes use the **top, right, bottom,** and **left** properties to specify position

- A **position : absolute** rule removes an element from the normal flow layout and positions it at a specified distance from the boundaries of its containing element

- The stacking order of overlapping elements can be specified by assigning integer values to their **z-index** property

- A **position : relative** rule moves an element from the position it would occupy in the normal flow layout and preserves the space it would have occupied

- A **position : fixed** rule removes an element from the normal flow layout and positions it at a specified distance from the boundaries of the viewport

- The **float** property accepts **left, right,** or **both** keywords to reposition an element within the normal flow layout and fill the space it would have occupied with content

- The **clear** property accepts **left, right,** or **both** keywords to explicitly prevent text flowing alongside a floated content box

- Overflowing content is **visible** by default but the **overflow** property can accept **hidden** or **scroll** keywords to specify alternative behavior

- The **clip** property accepts the **rect()** keyword that specifies the coordinates of a clipping area within its parentheses

- Web page authors are now discouraged from using HTML tables for layout as CSS provides a superior layout method

5 Formatting text

This chapter demonstrates how to suggest specific font styles for text content.

Suggesting a font

A CSS style rule can suggest a specific font to be used by the browser for the display of text content in a selected element by specifying the font name to its **font-family** property. The browser will use the specified font if it is available on the user's system – otherwise it will display the text using its default font.

The default font may not be the best choice for the author's purpose so CSS additionally allows the **font-family** property to suggest a generic font family from those in the table below:

Font Family :	Description :	Example :
serif	Proportional fonts where characters have different widths to suit their size, and with serif decorations at the end of the character strokes	**Times New Roman**
sans-serif	Proportional fonts without serif decorations	**Arial**
monospace	Non-proportional fonts where characters are of fixed width, similar to type-written text	**Courier**
cursive	Fonts that attempt to emulate human hand-written text	**Comic Sans**
fantasy	Decorative fonts with highly graphic appearance	**Castellar**

Hot tip

Develop the habit of enclosing all named fonts within quotes.

The browser will first try to apply the named font but in the event that it is unavailable will select a font from those available that most closely matches the characteristics of the generic preference. In this way the appearance of the text should at least approximate the author's intention, even without specific font-matching.

In a style rule **font-family** declaration the preferred font name should appear before the generic font family preference separated by a comma. Multiple named fonts can be specified as a comma-separated list – all before the generic font family preference. Font names that include spaces must be enclosed within quotes or they will not be recognized by the browser.

1 Create an HTML document containing a paragraph with several spanned sections of text

```
<p>The <span class="serif">City of New York</span>
was introduced to professional football on the same day
that the city was introduced to the
<span class="fantasy">New York Giants</span>.
It was a clear sunny
<span class="mono">October afternoon in 1925</span>
when the Giants took the field to play against the
<span class="cursive">Frankford Yellow Jackets</span>.
</p>
```

fontfamily.html

2 Save the HTML document then create a linked style sheet containing a rule suggesting a default font for the entire paragraph

```
p { font-family : "Arial Narrow", sans-serif }
```

fontfamily.css

3 Next add style rules suggesting fonts for the spanned text

```
span.serif { font-family : "Times New Roman", serif }
span.fantasy { font-family : "Castellar", fantasy }
span.mono { font-family : "Courier", monospace }
span.cursive { font-family : "Segoe Script", cursive }
```

4 Save the style sheet alongside the HTML document then open the web page in a browser to see the sections of text appear in the named fonts or generic family fonts

Don't forget

It is good practice to specify a generic font family preference in every **font-family** declaration.

77

Specifying font size

CSS provides a number of ways to specify the size of text in a style rule declaration by assigning values to the **font-size** property. The most obvious is as an absolute size using any of the absolute units listed on page 42. For example, as a **12pt** size like this:

#text-1 { font-size : 12pt }

Additionally CSS provides the keywords **xx-small, x-small, small, medium, large, x-large,** and **xx-large** to specify an absolute size.

Keyword :	Equivalent :
xx-large	24pt
x-large	17pt
large	13.5pt
medium	12pt
small	10.5pt
x-small	7.5pt
xx-small	7pt

Here the **medium** size is determined by the browser's default font size then the rest are computed relative to that size.

Where the default size is equivalent to **12pt** the computed values might look something like those in the table on the left.

So a style rule might specify a font size one scale higher than the default font size like this:

#text-2 { font-size : large }

Declarations may also specify a font size one scale higher or lower using the **larger** and **smaller** keywords like this:

#text-3 { font-size : larger }

Alternatively font size can be specified as a relative size using any of the relative units listed on page 42. For example, double the inherited size (or default size if none is inherited) like this:

#text-4 { font-size : 2em }

Similarly, font size can be specified as a relative size stated as a percentage. For example, as five times the inherited or default size with a style rule declaration like this:

#text-5 { font-size : 500% }

Hot tip

Use relative values rather than absolute values to specify font sizes for maximum flexibility.

1 Create an HTML document containing a paragraph with several spanned sections of text

```
<p>This 12pt high text can become
<span class = "lg">larger</span> or
<span class = "sm">smaller</span> <br>It can get
<span class = "xxl">extremely large</span> or
<span class = "xxs">extremely small</span> <br>
and it may even grow to be
<span class = "huge">huge</span>
</p>
```

fontsize.html

2 Save the HTML document then create a linked style sheet containing a rule specifying a default font size for the entire paragraph

```
p { font-size : 12pt }
```

fontsize.css

3 Next add style rules specifying font sizes for the spanned sections of text

```
span.lg { font-size : larger }
span.sm { font-size : smaller }
span.xxl { font-size : xx-large }
span.xxs.{ font-size : xx-small }
span.huge { font-size : 500% }
```

4 Save the style sheet alongside the HTML document then open the web page in a browser to see the sections of text appear in the specified font sizes

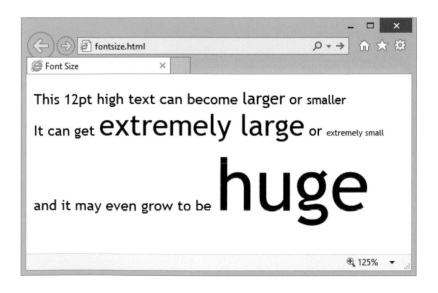

Adjusting font weight

The thickness or "weight" of text can easily be adjusted using the CSS **font-weight** property and the **bold** and **normal** keywords.

Specifying a **bold** value to a selected element's **font-weight** property causes normally-weighted text to appear in a heavier font and specifying a **normal** value causes heavily-weighted text to appear in a lighter font. In actuality the browser uses two different fonts to achieve this effect – for **normal** text it uses a regularly-weighted font (for example "Verdana") but it switches to the heavier-weighted variant of that font if one is available (such as "Verdana Bold") for **bold** text.

As an alternative to the bold and normal keywords a font weight can be specified as a numeric value from 100-900, by hundreds. A **font-weight** value of **400** is equivalent to **normal** weight and a value of **700** is equivalent to **bold** weight.

It is intended that this numeric weighting system should allow for font variants other than the **normal** and **bold** ones to be allotted to intermediate values. For example, a font lighter than the **normal** font (say, "Verdana Light") could equate to the weight value **300**. Similarly, a font heavier than the **bold** font (say, "Verdana Bold Black") could equate to the numeric weight value **800**.

In practice, however, the numeric system typically uses the **normal** font for values of **100, 200, 300, 400, 500** and the **bold** font for values of **600, 700, 800, 900**.

CSS also provides the keywords **bolder** and **lighter** for the purpose of moving up or down the font-weight ladder by single steps – but where the browser only recognizes two fonts, one for normal text and the other for bold text, these simply have the same effect as the **normal** and **bold** keywords.

fontweight.html

1 Create an HTML document with two paragraphs containing spanned sections of text

```
<p id = "para-1">This normal weight text can become
<span class = "bold">bold</span> or
<span class = "more">bolder</span>
</p>

<p id = "para-2">This bold weight text can get
<span class = "norm">light</span> or
<span class = "less">lighter</span>
</p>
```

2 Now add a heading containing a spanned section of text
```
<h2>...here's a heading with
<span class = "less">lighter</span> text</h2>
```

3 Save the HTML document then create a linked style sheet containing rules specifying a default font weight for each paragraph
```
p#para-1 { font-weight : 400 }
p#para-2 { font-weight : 700 }
```

fontweight.css

4 Next add style rules specifying font weights for the spanned sections of text
```
span.bold { font-weight: bold }
span.more { font-weight: bolder }
span.norm { font-weight: normal }
span.less { font-weight: lighter }
```

5 Save the style sheet alongside the HTML document then open the web page in a browser to see the sections of text appear in the specified font weights

Varying font styles

Slanting text

A CSS **font-style** property can request the browser to use a slanting variant of the current font by specifying the **italic** or **oblique** keywords – these are subtly different. When the **italic** keyword is specified the browser seeks an italicized variant of the current font in its font database. This is an actual font set, similar to the current upright font but graphically different to produce slanting versions of each upright character. When the **oblique** keyword is specified the browser seeks an oblique variant of the current font in its font database. This may be an actual font set, a slanting version of the current upright font, or alternatively it may be a generated version in which the browser has computed a slanting version of the upright font. Either may be mapped to the **oblique** keyword in the browser font database and called upon by the CSS **font-style** property. In reality using either **italic** or **oblique** keywords typically produces the same italicized text appearance, and in each case upright text can be resumed by specifying the **normal** keyword to the element's **font-style** property.

Small capitals

A CSS property called **font-variant** can specify a **small-caps** value to allow text characters to be displayed in a popular format using uppercase characters of two different sizes. Uppercase text in the selected element will appear as large capital characters but lowercase text will appear as smaller capitals. The browser may achieve this effect using a smaller capital from the font set, or by generating a computed smaller version. Once again regular text can be resumed by specifying the **normal** keyword as the **font-variant**.

<!-- HTML -->

fontstyle.html

1   Create an HTML document with two paragraphs and a heading containing spanned sections of text

```
<p id = "para-1">This normal style text can become
<span class = "ital">italicized</span> or
<span class = "oblq">oblique</span> </p>

<p id = "para-2">This italic style text can become
<span class = "reg">normal</span> </p>

<h2>...And Here's a
<span class="reg-caps">Heading</span>
with Small Caps</h2>
```

2 Save the HTML document then create a linked style sheet containing rules specifying default font styles for each paragraph
p#para-1 { font-style : normal }
p#para-2 { font-style : italic }

fontstyle.css

3 Next add style rules specifying font styles for the spanned sections of text in the paragraphs
span.ital { font-style: italic }
span.oblq { font-style: oblique }
span.reg { font-style: normal }

4 Now add style rules specifying font variants for the heading and its spanned text
h2 { font-variant: small-caps }
span.reg-caps { font-variant : normal }

5 Save the style sheet alongside the HTML document then open the web page in a browser to see the sections of text appear in the specified font styles and variants

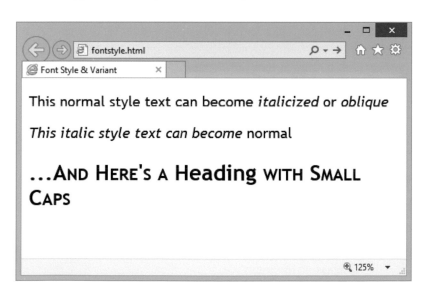

Using the font shorthand

Usefully CSS provides a **font** property to which various font preferences can be specified in a combined single rule stating:

font-style | font-variant | font-weight | font-size | font-family

Appropriate values can be assigned to each part of the combined **font** shorthand property. For example, like this:

p { font : italic small-caps bold medium "Times", serif }

The first three values for the **font-style, font-variant,** and **font-weight** properties may appear in any order. Optionally values for each one of these properties may be completely omitted and a **normal** value will be automatically assumed.

It is important to recognize that values not explicitly specified will still have a **normal** value applied – no value is inherited from the containing element, and this can produce some unexpected results. For example, a style rule selecting a span element within a containing paragraph element styled by the rule above might look like this:

span { font : large cursive }

The values explicitly specified in this rule will be applied to the **font-size** and **font-family** properties of the span element, and a **normal** value will be applied to its **font-style, font-variant,** and **font-weight** properties – so text within the span element does not inherit the **italic, small-caps,** or **bold** values from the paragraph.

One further possibility available with a combined **font** rule is the option to specify a **line-height** (the spacing between each line) by adding a forward slash and unit value after the **font-weight** value. This is useful to establish a common standard line spacing where various font sizes appear.

Beware

Remember that a **normal** value is applied for each part of a combined **font** rule unless explicitly specified – and this will override the current parent element value.

84

HTML

font.html

1. Create an HTML document containing a paragraph with several spanned sections of text
```
<p class = "general">
<span class = "header">The Sneakers Game</span><br>
In 1934 the
<span class = "giant">New York Giants</span> beat the
<span class="bears">Chicago Bears</span>, by
<span class = "score">30-13</span>,
in nine-degree temperatures
[ <span class="stadium">at the Polo Grounds</span> ]
```

in a game that has become famous as the "Sneakers Game." With the <span class ="giant">Giants</span> trailing <span class = "score">10-3</span> at the half, head coach <span class = "coach">Steve Owen</span> provided his squad with basketball shoes to increase traction on the icy turf. The team responded with four touchdowns in the second half to turn the game into a <span class = "giant">Giants</span> rout. </p>

2   Save the HTML document then create a linked style sheet with rules for the paragraph and span elements

```
p.general { font : normal small/1.3em "Courier", monospace }
span.header { font : 350% "Pristina", cursive }
span.giant { font : small-caps large "Castellar", fantasy }
span.bears { font : large "Arial", sans-serif }
span.score { font : bold small "Verdana", sans-serif }
span.stadium { font : italic medium "Arial", sans-serif }
span.coach { font : medium "Comic Sans MS", cursive }
```

font.css

3   Save the style sheet alongside the HTML document then open the web page in a browser to see the font styles

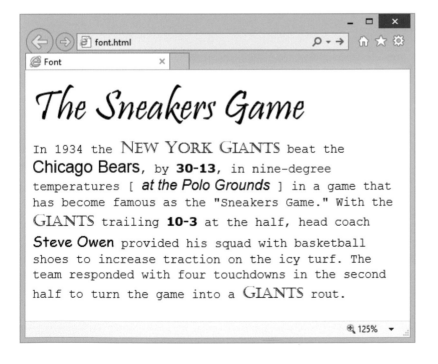

Hot tip

Always use the **font** shorthand property rather than the individual **font-style**, **font-variant**, **font-weight**, **font-size**, and **font-family** properties.

Aligning text

English language text in a paragraph is normally horizontally aligned to the left edge of the paragraph and this is the default behavior to display text in a paragraph element's content box.

Additionally CSS provides a **text-align** property that can explicitly specify how text should be aligned horizontally within the paragraph element's content box using the keywords **left**, **center**, **right**, or **justify**. As expected the **left** value aligns each line to the paragraph's left edge, the **right** value aligns each line to the paragraph's right edge, and the **center** value aligns each line centrally between both edges.

Perhaps more interestingly the **justify** value aligns each full line to both left and right edges of the content box and adjusts the spacing between characters and words to make each line the same length.

In displaying lines of text the browser automatically computes the line height to suit the content size – typically this will be the height of the font x 1.2. The browser then displays the text centered vertically in invisible "line boxes" of the computed height.

The CSS **vertical-align** property can explicitly specify how text should be aligned vertically using the keywords **baseline**, **sub**, and **super**. The **baseline** value specifies central vertical alignment, the default behavior. The **sub** and **super** values increase the boundaries of the outer container in which the line box exists and shift the text down or up respectively to display subscript or superscript.

Content can also be shifted up or down by specifying positive or negative unit values, or percentage values, to the **vertical-align** property. Alternatively the **top**, **middle**, and **bottom** keywords can specify vertical alignment with top-most, middle, or bottom-most content.

Two other keywords of **text-top** and **text-bottom** can be specified to the **vertical-align** property in order to vertically align other inline content boxes, such as those of image elements, to the top or bottom edge of a line box.

Don't forget

The **text-align** property only controls alignment of text within a content box – it is not used to center content boxes. See page 58 for details on how to center content boxes.

Hot tip

Usually subscript and superscript is much smaller than the text – create the vertical shift by specifying **sub** or **super** values then apply a **font** rule to reduce the shifted text's size.

1 Create an HTML document containing three paragraphs
```
<p>Enjoy the sunsets, the restaurants, the fishing, the
diving... the lifestyle of the Florida Keys!</p>

<p id="equalize">Enjoy the sunsets, the restaurants, the
fishing, the diving... the lifestyle of the Florida Keys!</p>

<p>Line <span class="up">Superscript</span>
<span class="down">Subscript</span>
<span class="top">Top</span></p>
```

align.html

2 Save the HTML document then create a linked style sheet containing a rule to specify the font and colors
```
p, span { font : medium monospace ;
          background : yellow ; border : 1px solid red }
```

align.css

3 Next add a rule to horizontally justify the text within the second paragraph's content box
```
p#equalize { text-align : justify }
```

4 Now add rules to adjust the vertical alignment of spanned text within the third paragraph
```
span.up { vertical-align : super }
span.down { vertical-align : sub }
span.top { vertical-align : top }
```

5 Save the style sheet alongside the HTML document then open the web page in a browser to see the alignments

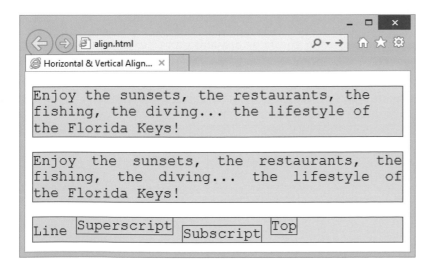

Indenting & spacing text

One of the most common features of printed text is the indentation of the first line of each paragraph to improve readability. This can easily be accomplished for text in HTML paragraphs using the **text-indent** property to specify an indentation size, such as **5em**.

Alternatively the indentation value may be specified as a percentage where the browser will indent an amount relative to the total line length. For example, given a paragraph element within a "div" container element of **500px** width, specifying a **text-indent** value of **10%** would indent the start of the first line by **50px** (500 x 10% = 50).

It is also possible to specify negative values for the **text-indent** property but this can produce inconsistent results so is best avoided.

The amount of space between each word can be adjusted from the **normal** default spacing by explicitly specifying a value to the CSS **word-spacing** property. Note that the specified value is added to the default spacing to increase the space. For example, specifying a unit value of **5em** increases the space to **normal+5em**, not a spacing of **5em** overall.

Similarly the amount of space between each letter can be adjusted from the **normal** default spacing by explicitly specifying a value to the CSS **letter-spacing** property. This also adds the specified value onto the default spacing to determine the total space. For example, specifying a unit value of **5em** increases the space to **normal+5em**, not a spacing of **5em** overall.

Both **word-spacing** and **letter-spacing** properties accept the **normal** keyword to resume normal spacing. Also they may both be overridden by the **text-align** property, described on the previous page, that has precedence in determining the appearance of the entire line.

① Create an HTML document with two paragraphs containing spanned text

```
<p>The Geologic Story at the
<span class="spread">Grand Canyon</span>
attracts the attention of the world for many reasons, but
perhaps its greatest significance lies in the geologic record
preserved and exposed here.</p><p>The rocks at
<span class="spread">Grand Canyon</span>
are not inherently unique but the
<span class="space">variety of rocks clearly exposed
present a complex geologic story.</span> </p>
```

space.html

② Save the HTML document then create a linked style sheet containing a rule to indent the start of each paragraph

p { text-indent : 5em }

space.css

③ Next add a style rule to increase the letter spacing and set a background color on two spanned sections of text

span.spread { letter-spacing : 1em ; background : yellow }

④ Now add a style rule to increase the word spacing and set a background color on the other spanned text

span.space { word-spacing : 1.5em ; background : aqua }

⑤ Save the style sheet alongside the HTML document then open the web page in a browser to see the indentations and spacing

Decorating text

Style rules can add decorative lines to text content using the CSS **text-decoration** property with keywords **underline**, **overline**, and **line-through**. These behave as expected adding a line below, a line above, and a line through the text respectively.

The **blink** keyword may also be specified to the **text-decoration** property to cause the browser to repeatedly hide then display the text, blinking it on and off.

More usefully, the CSS **none** keyword can be specified to the **text-decoration** property to prevent unwanted decorations appearing – this is particularly popular for displaying hyperlinks without their usual default underline.

Multiple keywords can be specified to the **text-decoration** property as a space-separated list to apply multiple decorations to the text.

An additional way to enhance text with CSS is available using the **text-transform** property to specify capitalization in the selected element with the keywords **uppercase**, **lowercase**, or **capitalize**.

Don't forget

Some users may not recognize hyperlinks if their default underline is removed.

decor.html

1. Create an HTML document with a paragraph containing spanned text and another paragraph containing hyperlinks, separated by a ruled line

```
<p id="para-1">You know that it's
<span class = "under caps">important</span>
when<br>it is
<span class = "under">underlined</span>
<br>and that it's been
<span class = "thru caps">cancelled</span>
when<br>it has been
<span class = "thru">struck through</span>
<br>but you also must remember to<br>
<span class = "rails upper">read between the lines</span>
<br>
<span id = "sig" class = "lower"> - MIKE MCGRATH</span>
</p>

<hr>

<p>
<a href = "http://w3c.org">Regular link</a> |
<a class = "plain" href = "http://w3c.org">Plain link</a>
</p>
```

2 Save the HTML document then create a linked style sheet with rules to specify fonts and colors

#para-1 { font : medium "Courier", monospace ;
                                    background : #CCCCFF }
#sig { font : xx-large "Lucida Handwriting", cursive ;
                                    color : purple }

decor.css

3 Next add style rules to decorate spanned text with lines

span.under { text-decoration : underline }
span.thru { text-decoration : line-through }
span.rails { text-decoration : overline underline blink }

4 Now add style rules to transform the case of spanned text

span.lower { text-transform : lowercase }
span.upper { text-transform : uppercase }
span.caps { text-transform : capitalize }

5 Finally add a style rule to remove the default underline from a hyperlink

a.plain { text-decoration : none }

6 Save the style sheet alongside the HTML document then open the web page in a browser to see the text decorations and case transformations

Beware

Avoid using the **blink** value as blinking text is despised by many users, and is not supported by default in some browsers.

Governing space & direction

The default treatment of whitespace within text content is to collapse multiple spaces into a single space, but this can be controlled with the CSS **white-space** property. Specifying the **pre** keyword preserves all spaces as they appear in the original text, including any line breaks. Conversely, the automatic wrapping of text in a block can be prevented by specifying the **no-wrap** keyword. Additionally the **pre-wrap** keyword can be specified to preserve spaces while still allowing text to wrap normally, or the **pre-line** keyword can be specified to collapse multiple spaces while preserving line breaks.

The default left-to-right direction of text lines can be changed to right-to-left by specifying the **rtl** keyword to the CSS **direction** property and the normal direction resumed with the **ltr** keyword.

Interestingly, when the line direction is changed with the **rtl** keyword the words appear from right-to-left but the order of English language characters is preserved so that each word still reads correctly left-to-right.

This intelligent feature also allows text to be presented in different directions on a single line. For example, to incorporate words in languages that are read right-to-left such as Hebrew and Arabic. The browser examines the Unicode value of each character using a complex BiDirectional algorithm to determine which direction each word should be displayed – those characters from right-to-left languages are automatically displayed in that direction, even if written logically from left-to-right in the HTML source code. The automatic BiDirectional algorithm can be turned off however by specifying the **bidi-override** keyword to a **unicode-bidi** property.

Hot tip

You can discover more about Unicode online at **www.unicode.org** and more on character entities at **www.w3.org**.

direction.html

1. Create an HTML document with a paragraph containing Hebrew character entities and stepped whitespace
```
<p>Hebrew "Congratulations" with mazel tov:
&#1502;&#1494;&#1500;  [mazel]
  + &#1496;&#1493;&#1489;  [tov]
    = &#1502;&#1494;&#1500;  &#1496;&#1493;&#1489;
</p>
```

2. Next begin a definition list with the same entities
```
<dl>
<dt>LTR Default Direction (lines begin at the LEFT):</dt>
<dd class = "ltr">&#1502;&#1494;&#1500; [mazel]
&#1496;&#1493;&#1489; [tov]</dd>
```

3 Now add two more definitions to complete the list, again featuring the same Hebrew character entities

```
<dt>RTL Custom Direction (lines begin at the RIGHT):</dt>
<dd class = "rtl">&#1502;&#1494;&#1500; [mazel]
&#1496;&#1493;&#1489; [tov]</dd>
<dt>LTR Explicit Direction + BiDirectional Override:</dt>
<dd class = "bidi-off ltr">No longer reads as mazel tov :
&#1502;&#1494;&#1500; &#1496;&#1493;&#1489;;</dd>
</dl>
```

4 Save the HTML document then create a linked style sheet with style rules to color element backgrounds and preserve whitespace in paragraphs

```
p,dd { background : yellow }
p { whitespace : pre }
```

direction.css

5 Now add style rules to set the text directions of each definition in the list

```
dd.ltr { direction : ltr }
dd.rtl { direction : rtl }
dd.bidi-off { unicode-bidi : bidi-override }
```

6 Save the style sheet alongside the HTML document then open the web page in a browser to see the preserved whitespace and various text directions

Beware

Generally the default treatment of right-to-left language characters achieves the desired effect. In practice overriding the Unicode BiDirectional algorithm is seldom needed.

Summary

- The **font-family** property can suggest specific fonts by name and also specify a generic font family as **serif, sans-serif, monospace, cursive,** or **fantasy**

- Font size can be specified using keywords such as **large,** absolute sizes such as **12pt,** or relative sizes such as **larger**

- Thickness of text can be specified to the **font-weight** property using keywords such as **bold,** or numeric values such as **700**

- Slanting text can be created by specifying the **italic** or **oblique** keywords to the **font-style** property

- Specifying a **small-caps** value to the **font-variant** property causes lowercase characters to appear as small capital letters

- The **font** shorthand property can be used to specify values for the **font-style, font-variant, font-weight, font-size,** and **font-family** properties rather than individual rules

- The **font-weight** property may also specify a **line-height** by adding a forward slash and unit size after the weight value

- Horizontal position of text within a content box can be specified to the **text-align** property by keywords such as **center**

- Vertical inline position of text can be specified to the **vertical-align** property using keywords such as **super**

- The **text-indent** property allows the start of each paragraph to be indented by a specified distance

- Text spacing can be adjusted by the **word-spacing** and **letter-spacing** properties

- Lines can be added to text by the **text-decoration** property and the case can be specified to the **text-transform** property

- Specifying **pre** to the **white-space** property preserves spacing

- The **direction** property can control text direction but can be overridden by the **unicode-bidi** property

6 Arranging data

This chapter demonstrates how to arrange data in tables and lists.

Setting table columns

Although web page authors are now discouraged from using HTML tables for page layout (in favor of CSS) tables remain an invaluable format for the presentation of information within the content of a page.

When displaying an HTML table the browser will, by default, automatically create a table layout sized to accommodate its content. This invariably produces a table with columns of varying width where each column width is determined by the widest content of any cell in that column. This process requires the browser to examine the table content in some detail before it can compute the optimum table layout and, especially for large tables, can take some time before the browser is able to draw the table.

CSS provides an alternative that allows the browser to quickly compute a suitable table layout without examining the content of the entire table – a fixed-layout can be specified to the **table-layout** property of a table element with the **fixed** keyword.

In a **fixed** layout the browser need only consider the **width** value of the table itself and the **width** value of the columns and cells on its first row to determine the table layout like this:

- The overall table width will be its specified **width** value or the sum of its column **width** values – whichever is the greater

- A specified column **width** value sets the width for that column

- When there is no specified column **width** value a specified cell **width** value sets the width for that column

- Any columns that have no specified **width** values, for either column or cell, will be sized equally within the table width

Alternatively a style rule can explicitly specify that the default table layout scheme should be used, in which the browser computes the column widths according to their content, by assigning an **auto** value to the **table-layout** property.

Where tables include a caption element the position of the caption can be suggested by specifying keywords of **top** or **bottom** to the table element's CSS **caption-side** property.

1 Create an HTML document containing two tables with similar content

```
<table><caption>Auto Layout</caption>
<tr><td>Text content</td>
<td>Text content wider than 130px</td>
<td>Text content</td></tr></table>

<table class = "fix"><caption>Fixed Layout</caption>
<tr><td>Text content</td>
<td>Text content wider than 130px</td>
<td>Text content</td></tr></table>
```

table.html

2 Save the HTML document then create a linked style sheet containing a rule to specify table width and its features

```
table { width : 500px ; border : 3px dashed blue ;
caption-side : top ; text-align : center ; margin : 0 0 20px }
```

table.css

3 Next add style rules to color each table cell and caption

```
td { border : 3px solid red ; background : yellow }
caption { background : aqua }
```

4 Now add a style rule to specify a fixed size column scheme for the second table

```
table.fix { table-layout : fixed }
```

5 Save the style sheet alongside the HTML document then open the web page in a browser to see tables drawn with both automatic and fixed layout schemes

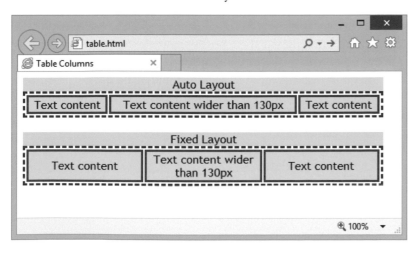

Spacing table cells

The distance between table cell borders can be specified as a unit value to the CSS **border-spacing** property. This easily allows cells to be spread some distance apart throughout a table.

A single specified **border-spacing** value will be applied uniformly to all cell separations – in much the same way as with the HTML **cellspacing** attribute.

CSS provides greater flexibility, however, by allowing two values to be specified to the **border-spacing** property as a space-separated list. The first will be applied to the horizontal spacing, at the left and right of each table cell, and the second will be applied to the vertical spacing at the top and bottom of each cell. This means that different distances can be specified for the horizontal and vertical spacing throughout a table.

Another possibility offered by CSS is the ability to hide table cells that contain no content. These frequently occur due to the grid format of tables, which does not always conveniently match the number of cells required. For example, displaying nine content items in a table of five rows and two columns.

Creating a style rule with the CSS **empty-cells** property specifying a **hide** value will cause the browser to not display the border and background of any cell that contains absolutely no content. Cells that contain any content at all, even if it's simply a ** ** (non-breaking space entity) will still be visible.

Conversely a style rule can explicitly ensure that empty cells are displayed by specifying a **show** value to the **empty-cells** property.

Empty cells that are hidden do continue to have a presence in the table layout inasmuch as their **border-spacing** values are preserved. For example, where the **border-spacing** property is set to **20px,** and the **empty-cells** property specifies a **hide** value, a single empty cell is not displayed but the surrounding cells remain 40 pixels apart – rather than just a distance of 20 pixels that would exist if the hidden cell did not exist.

1. Create an HTML document containing two tables with similar content

```
<table>
<tr><td>1</td><td></td><td>3</td></tr>
</table>

<table class = "space">
<tr><td>1</td><td></td><td>3</td></tr>
</table>
```

hide.html

2. Save the HTML document then create a linked style sheet containing a rule to specify table width and its features

```
table { width : 500px ;
               margin : 20px ; border : 3px dotted red }
```

hide.css

3. Next add a style rule to color each table cell and border

```
td { border : 3px solid blue ; background : aqua }
```

4. Now add a style rule to specify the border spacing and hide empty cells in the second table

```
table.space { border-spacing : 20px ; empty-cells : hide }
```

5. Save the style sheet alongside the HTML document then open the web page in a browser to see tables drawn with both visible and hidden empty cells

Collapsing table borders

The borders of adjacent table borders, and table cell borders, can be made to "collapse" into a single border by specifying the **collapse** keyword to the CSS **border-collapse** property. This requires the browser to perform a series of evaluations, comparing the existing borders, to determine how the collapsed border should appear:

- **Visibility Evaluation:** where one of the borders to be collapsed has a **border-style** value of **hidden,** that value takes precedence – so the collapsed border at that location will be hidden

- **Width Evaluation:** where two visible borders with different **border-width** values are to be collapsed, the highest value takes precedence – so the collapsed border will be the greater width

- **Style Evaluation:** where two visible borders of equal width are to be collapsed, their **border-style** value sets the precedence in the descending status order of **double, solid, dashed, dotted, ridge, outset, groove, inset** – so the collapsed border at that location will be in the style of highest status. For example, a **double** style wins out over a **solid** style

- **Color Evaluation:** where two visible borders of equal width and identical style are to be collapsed, the **border-color** value is determined in the descending status order of **cell, row, row group, column, column group, table** – so that collapsed border will be in the color of highest status. For example, the cell **border-color** wins out over the table **border-color** value

Don't forget

The **separate** keyword can also be specified to the **border-collapse** property – to explicitly prevent collapsing borders.

The effect of collapsing borders where a table **border-width** of **2px** is compared to a cell **border-width** of **5px** means that the collapsed **border-width** will be 5 pixels – the greater width.

In comparing adjacent **border-style** values of **dotted** and **double,** the collapsed **border-style** will be double – the higher status.

Similarly, comparing adjacent **border-style** values of **dotted** and **solid,** the collapsed **border-style** will be solid – the higher status.

1　Create an HTML document containing two tables with similar content

```
<table><tr>
<td class = "twin">1</td>
<td class = "dots">2</td>
<td class = "full">3</td> </tr></table>

<table class = "fold"><tr>
<td class = "twin">1</td>
<td class = "dots">2</td>
<td class = "full">3</td> </tr></table>
```

collapse.html

2　Save the HTML document then create a linked style sheet containing a rule to specify table width and its features

```
table { width : 500px ; height : 60px ; margin : 20px }
```

collapse.css

3　Next add style rules to specify the size and color of the table border and each table cell

```
table { border : 2px solid black }
td.twin { border : 5px double green }
td.dots { border : 5px dotted red }
td.full { border : 5px solid blue }
```

4　Now add a style rule to collapse the borders of the second table

```
table.fold { border-collapse : collapse }
```

5　Save the style sheet alongside the HTML document then open the web page in a browser to see tables drawn with both regular and collapsed borders

Assigning table features

The CSS **display** property can accept a range of values to specify that a selected element should be treated as a table component – emulating the default behavior of HTML tags that a browser automatically applies to table components:

HTML Tag :	CSS Equivalent :
<table>	table
<tr>	table-row
<thead>	table-header-group
<tbody>	table-row-group
<tfoot>	table-footer-group
<col>	table-column
<colgroup>	table-column-group
<th>	} table-cell
<td>	
<caption>	table-caption

The CSS values that can be specified to the **display** property are listed in the table above together with the HTML tag they most closely represent. These can be used to specify table features to elements of an XML document so a browser will display their content as if it was an HTML table.

xtable.xml

1. Create an XML document that nominates a CSS style sheet to format its element content

```
<?xml version="1.0" encoding="UTF-8"?>
<?xml-stylesheet href="xtable.css" type="text/css"?>
<liga><cap>La Liga Top 3</cap>
 <hdrs>
  <lbl>Position</lbl> <lbl>Team</lbl> <lbl>Points</lbl>
 </hdrs>
 <rows>
  <team> <pos>1</pos> <name>Barcelona</name>
  <pts>84</pts> </team>
  <team> <pos>2</pos> <name>Real Madrid</name>
  <pts>80</pts> </team>
  <team> <pos>3</pos> <name>Villareal</name>
  <pts>65</pts> </team>
 </rows>
</liga>
```

2 Save the XML document then create a linked style sheet with rules that assign table characteristics to the XML tags

```
cap { display : table-caption }
liga { display : table }
hdrs { display: table-header-group }
rows { display: table-row-group }
team { display: table-row }
name, pos,pts, lbl { display: table-cell }
```

xtable.css

3 Next add a style rule that specifies the table features

```
liga { margin : auto ; margin-top : 20px ; width : 300px ;
            border-spacing : 3px ; border : 8px ridge lime }
```

4 Now add style rules to color the headers and row cells

```
hdrs { background : lime }
rows { background: aqua }
```

5 Save the style sheet alongside the XML document then open the document in a browser to see the table

Position	Team	Points
1	Barcelona	84
2	Real Madrid	80
3	Villareal	65

La Liga Top 3

Choosing list markers

A list "marker" indicates the beginning of an item in a list – typically a bullet in an unordered <ul> list, or an incrementing number in an <ol> ordered list. The browser conducts an item count in each case but usually only uses this to number the items in an ordered list display.

The CSS **list-style-type** property can specify an alternative type of marker for any list – so unordered lists can have numbered markers and ordered lists can have bullet-points if so desired.

Keywords allow the bullet marker type to be specified as **disc**, **circle**, or **square**, and number marker types as **lower-roman**, **upper-roman**, **decimal**, or **decimal-leading-zero**.

Alphabetical marker types can be specified with the **lower-latin**, **upper-latin**, and **lower-greek** keywords. Additionally the CSS specification provides keywords for other alphabets such as **armenian** and **georgian** – but a suitable font is needed for the marker to be displayed correctly by the web browser.

The **list-style-type** property can also specify a **none** value to explicitly suppress the markers so they will not be displayed, although they do remain in the item count.

Optionally an image may be specified as a marker by stating its path in the parentheses of a **url()** value to the **list-style-image** property.

markers.html

1 Create an HTML document containing three headings and several ordered lists
```
<h3>Alphabetical list marker types:</h3>
<ol id = "list-0"><li>lower-latin<li>...<li>...</ol>
<ol id = "list-1"><li>upper-latin<li>...<li>...</ol>
<ol id = "list-2"><li>lower-greek<li>...<li>...</ol>
<h3>Bullet list marker types:</h3>
<ol id = "list-3"><li>disc<li>...<li>...</ol>
<ol id = "list-4"><li>circle<li>...<li>...</ol>
<ol id = "list-5"><li>square<li>...<li>...</ol>
<ol id = "list-6"><li>image<li>...<li>...</ol>
<h3>Numerical list marker types:</h3>
<ol id = "list-7"><li>lower-roman<li>...<li>...</ol>
<ol id = "list-8"><li>upper-roman<li>...<li>...</ol>
<ol id = "list-9"><li>decimal<li>...<li>...</ol>
<ol id = "list-10"><li>decimal-leading-zero<li>...<li>...</ol>
```

...cont'd

2 Save the HTML document then create a linked style sheet with rules to specify heading and list features
```
h3 { clear : left ; margin : 0 }
ol {margin : 0 ; border : 1px solid black ; float : left ;
    background : aqua ; padding : 0 0 0 10px }
li { margin : 0 0 0 20px ; background : yellow }
```

markers.css

3 Next add style rules to specify alphabetical list markers
```
ol#list-0 { list-style-type: lower-latin }
ol#list-1 { list-style-type: upper-latin }
ol#list-2 { list-style-type: lower-greek }
```

4 Now add style rules to specify bullet list markers
```
ol#list-3 { list-style-type: disc}
ol#list-4 { list-style-type: circle }
ol#list-5 { list-style-type: square }
ol#list-6 { list-style-image : url(tick.png) }
```

5 Finally add style rules to specify numerical list markers
```
ol#list-7 { list-style-type: lower-roman }
ol#list-8 { list-style-type: upper-roman }
ol#list-9 { list-style-type: decimal }
ol#list-10 { list-style-type: decimal-leading-zero }
```

6 Save the style sheet alongside the HTML document then open the web page in a browser to see the list markers

Don't forget

Both numerical and alphabetical markers display the incrementing item count.

105

Positioning list markers

Typically, to display a list the browser creates a block-level content box for the entire list and inline content boxes for each list item. Typically, a left margin insets the list item content boxes and each marker appears up against the right edge of this margin area – outside the list item content boxes.

The position of the marker may be explicitly specified to the **list-style-position** property using **inside** or **outside** keywords to determine whether the markers should appear inside the list item content boxes.

Rather than creating separate style rules for the **list-style-type**, **list-style-image**, and **list-style-position** properties it is simpler to use the CSS shorthand technique that may specify a value for each property as a space-separated list to the **list-style** property. The values may appear in any order and where any value is omitted the default value for that property will be assumed.

Lists of either type may be nested with their marker position and type specified independently.

list.html

1 Create an HTML document containing three lists plus one nested list
```
<ol class = "outside-markers">
 <li>List<li>Markers<li>Outside content box
</ol>

<ol class =  "inside-markers">
 <li>List<li>Markers<li>Inside content box
</ol>

<ul>
 <li>List<li>Style
 <ol class =  "inside-markers">
 <li>List<li>Markers<li>Inside content box
 </ol><li>Shorthand
</ul>
```

list.css

2 Save the HTML document then create a linked style sheet containing rules to show the list boundaries
```
li { background : yellow }
ol,ul { border : 2px solid red }
```

3 Next add a style rule to specify that some ordered list markers should appear outside the list item content boxes
ol.outside-markers { list-style-position : outside }

4 Now add a style rule to specify that other ordered list markers should appear inside the list item content boxes
ol.inside-markers { list-style-position : inside }

5 Finally add a shorthand style rule that specifies the position, image, and bullet type for the unordered list
ul { list-style : url(lilguy.png) outside square }

6 Save the style sheet alongside the HTML document then open the web page in a browser to see the lists

Hot tip

Nested lists can specify they should adopt the **list-style** of the containing element using the **inherit** keyword or suppress markers with the **none** keyword.

Don't forget

The **square** marker type specified by the shorthand rule will be used when the specified image is not available.

107

Summary

- When the **table-layout** property specifies a **fixed** layout the browser need only assess the **width** value of the table and the **width** of the cells on its first row so it can quickly draw the table

- The **caption-side** property can specify whether the table caption should appear at the **top** or **bottom** of the table

- A **border-spacing** property can specify the distance between table cell borders

- Cells containing absolutely no content can be hidden by specifying a **hide** value to the **empty-cells** property

- Adjacent borders of a table and its cells can be combined into a single border by specifying the **collapse** keyword to the **border-collapse** property

- The **display** property can specify that a selected element should be treated by the browser as a table component using **table, table-row, table-header-group, table-row-group, table-cell, table-footer-group, table-column,** or **table-caption** keywords

- A **list-style-type** property can specify the type of bullet marker to be used for list items with **disc, circle,** or **square** keywords

- The **list-style-type** property can specify that each list item should have numerical markers using the **lower-roman, upper-roman, decimal,** or **decimal-leading-zero** keywords

- Alphabetical list markers can be specified to the **list-style-type** property as **lower-latin, upper-latin,** or **lower-greek**

- An image can be used as a list marker by stating its path in the **url()** value specified to the **list-style-image** property

- Specifying a value of **inside** or **outside** to the **list-style-position** determines whether markers appear inside the content box

- The **list-style** property can specify the individual **list-style-type, list-style-image,** and **list-style-position** properties as CSS shorthand

7 Generating effects

This chapter demonstrates how to generate content and create dynamic effects.

Inserting text enhancements

CSS provides four "pseudo-elements" of **:before**, **:after**, **:first-letter**, and **:first-line** that can be included in the style rule selector to enhance the actual content of a selected element.

The **:before** and **:after** pseudo-elements place generated content around the original content and appear in the selector immediately after the element name. For example, a selector of **p:before** generates content before the content of each paragraph.

The **:before** and **:after** pseudo-elements specify the content to be generated to a **content** property in the style rule declaration. Most simply the declaration specifies a string of text to be generated. The string must be enclosed within quote marks though these will not be included in the generated content, but spaces in the string will be preserved in the generated content. Alternatively the **content** property can specify the keywords **open-quote** or **close-quote** to explicitly generate quotes around original content.

Generated content is not limited to text strings, as the special **url()** keyword can be used to specify non-textual content to the **content** property by stating the path to a resource within the parentheses. For example, a declaration might specify an image to be generated using **content : url(image.png)** to generate the image as content.

Additionally the special **attr()** keyword can be used to specify to the **content** property the name of an attribute within the selected element whose assigned value should be generated as content. For example, a declaration might specify an attribute whose value should be generated using **content : attr(src)** to generate the value of the selected element's "src" attribute as content.

Multiple items to be generated can be specified to the **content** property as a space-separated list – using any of the above.

pseudo.html

1. Create an HTML document with five paragraphs that each contain a hyperlink to the same resource
```
<p>Get more <a href = "info.pdf">info</a> here</p>
<p>Get more
   <a href = "info.pdf" class = "quo">info</a> here</p>
<p>Get more
   <a href = "info.pdf" class = "lnk">info</a> here</p>
<p>Get more
   <a href = "info.pdf" class = "pdf">info</a> here</p>
<p>Get more
   <a href = "info.pdf" class = "att">info</a> here</p>
```

2 Save the HTML document then create a linked style
sheet containing rules to add text characters on colored
backgrounds before and after the content of each paragraph
p:before { content : "*" ; background : yellow }**
p:after { content : "!!!" ; background : aqua }

pseudo.css

3 Next add rules to insert colored quotes around a link
a[href].quo:before { content : open-quote ; color : red }
a[href].quo:after { content : close-quote ; color : red }

4 Now add a rule to insert colored text before a link
a[href].lnk:before { content : "[link]: " ; color : orange }

5 Then add a rule to insert an image after a link
a[href].pdf:after { content : url(pdf-ico.png) }

6 Finally add a rule to insert a colored attribute value after
a link
a[href].att:after { content : " [" attr(href) "] " ;
**   color : green }**

7 Save the style sheet alongside the HTML document
then open the web page in a browser to see the content
generated by CSS in addition to that in the HTML code

Hot tip

The **:first-letter** and
:first-line properties
target text content
within an element – an
example using these
pseudo-elements appears
on page 113.

111

Hot tip

Generated content
is added inside the
content box of the
selected element – so
the enhancements to
the links in this example
become part of the link.

Numbering document sections

The CSS :**before** pseudo-element, introduced in the previous example, can insert generated content to automatically number sections of an HTML document using the special **counter()** keyword. This specifies the name of a counter to be inserted into content within its parentheses.

A counter to count the instances of a selected element must first be created by specifying a chosen name and an incremental value to the **counter-increment** property as a space-separated list.

The counter will begin counting from zero by default and will increment by the specified incremental value for every instance of the selected element. Optionally the explicitly-specified incremental value may be omitted from the rule so the value of 1 will be assumed as the incremental value. For example, a declaration of **counter-increment : num** creates a counter named "num" that will start counting from zero and increment by one.

Additionally the counter can be made to resume counting from a number other than the current count number by specifying the counter name and an integer value from which to count as a space-separated list to the **counter-reset** property. Typically this will specify a zero integer value to resume counting afresh.

Once a counter has been created it can be inserted before a selected element as generated content by a CSS pseudo-element.

counter.html

1. Create an HTML document with various headings of two different sizes

```
<h2>Topic</h2>
    <h3>Section</h3>
    <h3>Section</h3>
    <h3>Section</h3>

<h2>Topic</h2>
    <h3 class="restart">Section</h3>
    <h3>Section</h3>
    <h3>Section</h3>
```

counter.css

2. Save the HTML document then create a linked style sheet containing a rule to create a counter for the larger heading elements, which will increment by one
h2 { counter-increment : num 1 }

3 Next add a style rule to create a counter for the smaller heading elements, which will increment by one
h3 { counter-increment : sub 1 }

4 Now add a style rule to insert the current larger heading counter value before each larger heading and set the counter's background color
h2:before { content : counter(num) " " ;
                                          background : aqua }

5 Then add a style rule to insert both the current larger and smaller heading counter value before each smaller heading and set that background color
h3:before { content : counter(num) "." counter(sub) " " ;
                                        background : lime }

6 Finally add a style rule to reset the smaller heading counter after each larger heading element
h3.restart { counter-reset : sub 0 }

7 Save the style sheet alongside the HTML document then open the web page in a browser to see the generated counter values inserted before each heading

Counter Numbering

1 Topic

    1.1 Section

    1.2 Section

    1.3 Section

2 Topic

    2.1 Section

    2.2 Section

    2.3 Section

                                                      100% ▼

Hot tip

Notice that, for formatting purposes, the generated content in this example includes a space.

Highlighting important content

In addition to the four pseudo-elements of :**before**, :**after**, :**first-letter**, and :**first-line**, CSS provides a number of pseudo-classes that can be included with the selector in a style rule.

Typically the :**first-child** and :**lang()** pseudo-classes are used to highlight content by changing the text color or background color. It is important to recognize that the :**first-child** pseudo-class acts upon the first selected element contained within an outer element – not the first child element within a selected element.

The :**lang()** pseudo-class can be included in a style rule selector to select an element by its language as an alternative to using the attribute selector technique described on page 30. For example, the selector *:**lang(es)** is equivalent to the selector *[**lang="es"**] to select all elements that have a **lang** attribute assigned an "es" value denoting Spanish language content. The :**lang()** pseudo-class is more powerful, however, as it also considers other factors, such as document headers and meta data, to determine the language.

Notice that, unlike the attribute selector, the :**lang()** pseudo-class does not require quote marks around the language specified within its parentheses. Its simpler syntax and greater power make the :**lang()** pseudo-class the preferred method to select elements according to the language of their content.

Unlike pseudo-elements, multiple pseudo-classes can be included in a single selector. For example, **p:first-child:lang(fr)** would select the first paragraph element with French language content that is contained within an outer element.

The :**first-child** and :**lang()** pseudo-classes can often be used in conjunction with the :**first-letter** and :**first-line** pseudo-elements to highlight important content.

highlight.html

1   Create an HTML document with two paragraphs containing spanned sections of text
```
<p>In what was once Texcoco lake, birthplace of
<span>pre-Hispanic civilizations</span>, lies the
<span lang = "es">Ciudad de los Palacios</span>
(City of Palaces) that is today, Mexico City.</p>

<p>Mexico City offers visitors a great many different
interesting sites to visit, from
<span>pre-Columbian Mexico</span> to modern and
<span>cosmopolitan 21st century Mexico</span>.</p>
```

2   Save the HTML document then create a linked style
    sheet containg a rule to color the first letter of each paragraph
    p:first-letter { font-size : 200% ; color : red }

3   Next add a style rule to color the background of the first
    line in each paragraph
    p:first-line { background-color : yellow }

4   Now add a style rule to color the background of elements
    containing Spanish language content
    ***:lang(es) { background-color : lime }**

5   Finally add a style rule to color the first section of
    spanned text within an outer containing element
    span:first-child { background-color : aqua }

6   Save the style sheet alongside the HTML document then
    open the web page in a browser to see the highlighted
    content

highlight.css

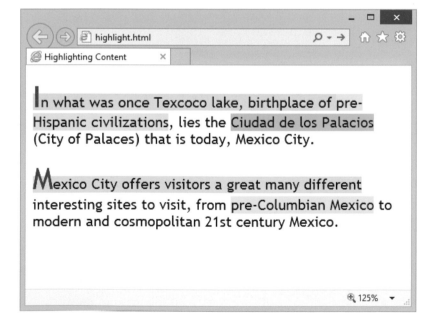

highlight.html

Highlighting Content

In what was once Texcoco lake, birthplace of pre-
Hispanic civilizations, lies the Ciudad de los Palacios
(City of Palaces) that is today, Mexico City.

Mexico City offers visitors a great many different
interesting sites to visit, from pre-Columbian Mexico to
modern and cosmopolitan 21st century Mexico.

125%

Hot tip

Notice that the
:first-child class has more
weight than the
:first-line element – so
part of the first line is
colored by the **:first-child**
rule's declaration.

Providing special cursors

The CSS **cursor** property can specify the type of cursor to display when the pointer hovers over a selected element. Its default value of **auto** allows the browser to determine which cursor to display, but specifying a **default** keyword will explicitly force the browser to use the operating system's default cursor.

Alternative cursor keywords, together with the cursor icons they represent in the Windows operating system, are listed below:

Keyword :	Cursor :	Keyword :	Cursor :
default	⬉	n-resize	↕
pointer	👆	ne-resize	⤢
crosshair	+	e-resize	↔
move	✛	se-resize	⬊
text	I	s-resize	↕
wait	⌛	sw-resize	⤢
progress	⬉⌛	w-resize	↔
help	⬉?	nw-resize	⬊

Traditionally the **pointer** cursor icon indicates a hyperlink, the **move** cursor icon indicates an item that can be dragged, and the **text** cursor icon indicates a component in which text can be selected. As most users are familiar with these cursor conventions it is best to adhere to them.

In addition to system cursor icons the **cursor** property can specify an image for use as a custom cursor icon by stating its path within the parentheses of the **url()** keyword. Multiple images may be specified, as a comma-separated list, but the list should always end with a regular cursor keyword to specify which system cursor icon to use if the specified images are unavailable.

...cont'd

1 Create an HTML document containing two paragraphs
```
<p class ="help-cursor">Browser defined help cursor</p>
<p class ="arrow-cursor">
        Custom arrow cursor (or browser default)</p>
```

cursor.html

2 Save the HTML document then create a linked style sheet with a rule to specify paragraph height and color
```
p { border : 1px solid black ; height : 50px ;
                        background: yellow }
```

cursor.css

3 Next add style rules to specify cursors for the paragraphs
```
p.help-cursor { cursor : help }
p.arrow-cursor{ cursor : url(blue-arrow.cur), default }
```

blue-arrow.cur

4 Save the style sheet alongside the HTML document then hover the pointer over each paragraph to see the cursors

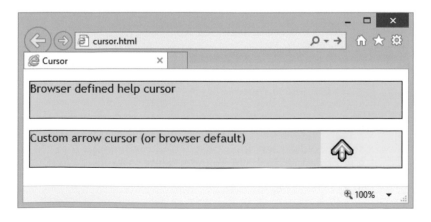

Outlining page components

Components of an HTML document can be emphasized using the CSS **outline** property to draw an outline around selected elements. Unusually, the outline is drawn around the content of the selected elements on a layer above the content box – so it does not influence the box model in any way.

The **outline** shorthand property is similar to the **border** shorthand property inasmuch as it can accept very nearly all the same values to specify style, width, and color, as a space-separated list.

As with the **border** property, a style must always be explicitly specified to the **outline** property but the width and color values may be omitted. There are also **outline-style**, **outline-width**, and **outline-color** properties to specify individual property values.

Unlike borders, outlines always have uniform style on each side – so there are no outline properties to specify individual side values, nor can the **outline-style** property have a **hidden** value.

In addition to specifying color in the usual way, the **outline-color** property can specify an **invert** keyword to have the browser select a color that contrasts with that behind the outline – so the outline will always be easily visible.

The CSS specifications leave the precise treatment of outlines to be determined by the browser but they do make suggestions as to how they may appear. Surprisingly, the truly unique suggestion is that an outline can be non-rectangular. This does not provide curved outlines (yet) but allows contiguous outlines to disappear leaving a single non-rectangular outline around the content edges.

The suggested position at which to draw an **outline**, relative to the box model beneath, is just outside the border edge.

outline.html

① Create an HTML document with one heading and a paragraph containing some spanned text
`<h2>Gold Rush Fever</h2>`

`<p>By early 1849, gold fever was an epidemic. <span>Farmers left their fields; merchants closed their shops; soldiers left their posts - and made plans for California.</span> Newspapers fanned the fires.</p>`

2 Save the HTML document then create a linked style sheet containing a rule to specify margin and padding values for the heading and paragraph elements
h2,p { padding : 5px ; width : 500px }

outline.css

3 Next add style rules to specify borders and backgrounds for the heading and paragraph elements
h2 { border : 3px dashed blue ; background : aqua }
p { border : 3px dashed green ; background : yellow }

4 Now add a style rule to add an outline around the spanned text
h2,span { outline : 2px solid red }

5 Save the style sheet alongside the HTML document then open the web page in a browser to see the text outlined

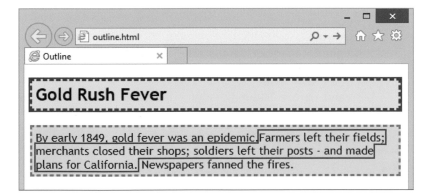

Beware

The CSS specifications do not define how overlapping lines should be treated so their appearance can vary. Notice the difference shown here between this example in Internet Explorer and Firefox.

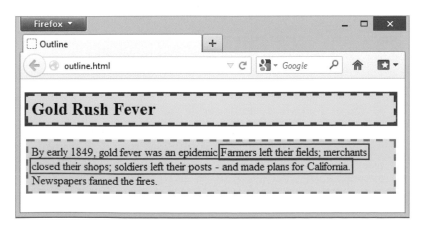

Indicating current focus

Interactive components of an HTML document comprise those elements that can accept keyboard input, such as a text field, and those that can be activated by a user action, such as a push button or hyperlink. When one of these interactive components is selected by the user, typically by a mouse click or tab key, it is ready to be activated and is said to have "focus".

CSS provides the **:focus** pseudo-class that can be used to apply styling to the element with current focus in a document – in recognition of the user's selection. The styling is removed from that element when the focus shifts to another element, as the user selects a different interactive component.

Indicating the element with current focus is especially useful in lengthy forms with many input fields, as it acts as a marker that easily identifies the progress through the form.

focus.html

1 Create an HTML document containing a form with several interactive components
```
<form action="">
<fieldset>
<legend> Send for details </legend>
<label for = "addr">Enter your email address: </label>
<input id = "addr" type = "text">
<input type = "submit" value = "Send">
<a href = "http://samples">Samples Page</a>
</fieldset>
</form>
```

focus.css

2 Save the HTML document then create a linked style sheet with a rule to color input elements when in focus
input:focus { background : lime }

3 Next add a style rule to color hyperlinks when in focus
a:focus { background : aqua }

4 Save the style sheet alongside the HTML document then open the web page in a browser and select each interactive component in turn to see the styles applied

...cont'd

121

Don't forget

Focus only relates to interactive elements that can receive keyboard input or somehow be activated by the user.

Displaying hyperlink status

Hyperlinks in an HTML document appear in the color designated by the browser's default scheme to indicate their status as either "visited" or "unvisited". The status is determined by comparing the user's browser history and typically uses the colors from Internet Explorer's default scheme, shown below:

122

The CSS **:link** and **:visited** pseudo-classes can be used to specify different colors to indicate the history status of hyperlinks in a document.

Additionally, the **:hover** and **:active** pseudo-classes can be used to specify explicit colors to indicate the interactive status of hyperlinks. The color specified to the **:hover** pseudo-class is applied when the link has focus, ready to be activated.

The color specified to the **:active** pseudo-class is applied when the user actually activates the link, usually by clicking the mouse button while the cursor hovers above the link.

It is important to recognize that the **:link** pseudo-class selects only those **<a>** anchor elements that include an **href** attribute, not fragment anchors that simply mark positions in a page.

link.html

1 Create an HTML document containing an ordered list in which each item is an anchor element
```
<ol>
<li><a name = "top">Fragment anchor</a>
<li><a href = "http://been-there">Visited link</a>
<li><a href = "http://go-there">Unvisited link</a>
</ol>
```

link.css

2 Save the HTML document then create a linked style sheet containing a rule to set anchor colors
a { color : blue }

3 Next add style rules to specify hyperlink status colors
a:link { color : red }
a:visited { color : gray }

4 Now add style rules to specify hyperlink interactive colors
a:hover { color : green }
a:active { color : orange }

5 Save the style sheet alongside the HTML document then open the web page in a browser and activate the hyperlinks to see the specified color in each state

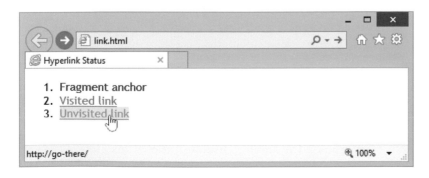

Hot tip

Remember the difference between the pseudo-classes. Both **:link** and **:visited** apply static styles but **:hover**, **:active** (and **:focus**) apply styles dynamically in response to user actions.

123

Reacting to user events

User actions cause interface "events" to which the three dynamic pseudo-classes **:focus**, **:hover**, and **:active** can react. For example, when a user clicks on a text input the Focus event occurs – to which the **:focus** pseudo-class can react by applying styles. Perhaps more interestingly, when the user moves the cursor onto any element the MouseOver event occurs – to which the **:hover** pseudo-class can react by applying styles. The applied styles are removed when the cursor moves off the element, as the MouseOut event occurs, creating a dynamic "rollover" effect.

Typically the rollover will highlight the selected element by changing its content color or background color to become more prominent. A rollover might also specify a different background image to create an image-swap – but this may not work too well on slower connections that need to wait for the new image to download.

A better image-swap alternative is to combine the images for both MouseOver and MouseOut states into a single image file, then have the rollover reveal the appropriate half of the image by specifying a different background position for each state.

rollover.png

 Create an image file of 150x100 pixels containing two images, one above the other, on a transparent background

rollover.html

2 Next create an HTML document containing two empty "div" elements with id attributes for style rule reference
<div id = "box-1"></div> <div id = "box-2"></div>

rollover.css

3 Save the HTML document then create a linked style sheet with rules to set the div elements' absolute position and size – with a height exactly half that of the image
div#box-1 { position : absolute ; top : 10px ; left : 10px ; width : 150px ; height : 50px }
div#box-2 { position : absolute ; top : 10px ; left: 170px ; width : 150px ; height : 50px }

4 Now add style rules to color the backgrounds and set the background position at the top left corner of the image, when the cursor is not over the div elements
div#box-1 { background-color : blue }
div#box-2 { background : url(rollover.png) 0px 0px aqua }

5 Finally add style rules to change the background colors and set the background position at the center left of the image, when the cursor is over the div elements
div#box-1:hover { background-color : red }
div#box-2:hover {
          background : url(rollover.png) 0px -50px lime }

6 Save the style sheet alongside the HTML document then open the web page in a browser and roll the cursor over the div elements to see their backgrounds change

Don't forget

The **:focus** pseudo-class only relates to elements that can receive input – but the **:hover** pseudo-class relates to ANY element.

Interacting with CSS buttons

A rollover effect, as described in the previous example, can be combined with a hyperlink to create a navigation "button" using dynamic pseudo-classes to style hyperlink anchor elements. It is generally desirable to nest the anchor element within an outer containing element of defined size, then apply a rule setting the **display** property of the anchor element to **block** – so it expands up to the boundaries of the containing element. This makes the entire area of the containing element "clickable" and the anchor element's background will fill the container. A vertical column of navigation buttons can easily be created as a definition list in which each list item is a button.

buttons.html

1 Create an HTML document containing a definition list with a hyperlink in each list item
```
<dl id = "menu">
<dt class="btn"><a href = "a.html">Button 1</a></dt>
<dt class="btn"><a href = "b.html">Button 2</a></dt>
<dt class="btn"><a href = "c.html">Button 3</a></dt>
</dl>
```

buttons.css

2 Save the HTML document then create a linked style sheet containing a rule to set the list position and size
```
dl#menu { position : absolute ;
                  top : 10px ; left : 20px ; width : 150px }
```

3 Next add a style rule to space the list items vertically and position their text content centrally
```
dt.btn { margin-bottom : 5px ; text-align : center }
```

4 Now add a style rule to expand the anchor elements to fill their containing list item content boxes, color the text, and suppress the default hyperlink underlines
```
dt.btn a { display : block ; color : white ;
                  font-weight : bold ; text-decoration : none }
```

5 Finally add style rules to color the buttons differently according to the hyperlink status
```
dt.btn a:link, a:visited
                  { background : blue ; border : 5px outset blue }
dt.btn a:hover
                  { background : red ; border : 5px outset red }
dt.btn a:active
                  { background : green ; border : 5px inset green }
```

6 Save the style sheet alongside the HTML document then open the web page in a browser to see the button appearance change in response to user actions

Don't forget

Applying a **display:block** style rule to the anchor elements is vital to the success of this effect.

Moving CSS tabs

In addition to changing the appearance of the selected element, to create a rollover effect, the three dynamic CSS pseudo-classes of **:focus**, **:hover**, and **:active** can apply styles that change the size or position of the selected element to create a further dynamic effect. For example, with absolutely-positioned elements a style rule can specify different offset values to reposition the selected element in response to a user action.

Alternatively the element size can be dynamically changed by specifying different values to its **padding** property. This is often a better option and can be used to create slide-out hyperlink tabs.

tabs.html

1 Create an HTML document containing a definition list with a hyperlink in each list item
```
<dl id = "menu">
<dt class="tab"><a href="a.html">Tab 1</a></dt>
<dt class="tab"><a href="b.html">Tab 2</a></dt>
<dt class="tab"><a href="c.html">Tab 3</a></dt>
</dl>
```

tabs.css

2 Save the HTML document then create a linked style sheet containing a rule to set the list position and size
```
dl#menu { position : absolute ;
                top : 0px ; left : 10px ; margin : 0 }
```

3 Next add a style rule to space the list items horizontally and position their text content centrally
```
dt.tab { display : block ; float : left ;
              margin-right : 5px ; text-align : center }
```

4 Now add a style rule to expand the anchor elements to fill their containing list item content boxes, color the text, and suppress the default hyperlink underlines
```
dt.tab a { display : block ; text-decoration : none ;
            color : white ; font-weight : bold ; width : 100px }
```

5 Finally add style rules to color the tabs differently and adjust their size according to the hyperlink status
```
dt.tab a { background : blue ; border : 5px outset blue }
dt.tab a:hover { padding-top :20px ; background : red ;
                                border-color : red }
dt.tab a:active { padding-top : 20px ; background : green ;
                                border-color : green }
```

6 Save the style sheet alongside the HTML document then open the web page in a browser to see the tab appearance and size change in response to user actions

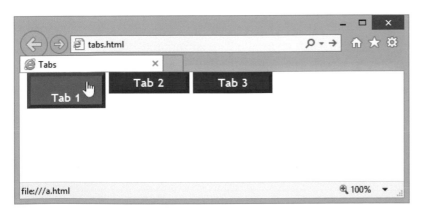

Beware

Use dynamic resizing with caution as it may hide other content unless all content is absolutely positioned to allow for resized content boxes.

Hiding & revealing elements

Besides the ability to style an element's appearance, position, and size, the three dynamic CSS pseudo-classes of **:focus**, **:hover**, and **:active** can control whether the selected element is even visible.

Specifying the **hidden** keyword to an element's **visibility** property will hide the element. Conversely a **hidden** element can be revealed by specifying the **visible** keyword to its **visibility** property.

Images placed on hidden elements that are absolutely positioned at the same coordinates can be revealed individually as the user places the cursor over scaled-down "thumbnail" versions of each image – to produce a more compact page.

visibility.html

1   Create an HTML document containing a definition list with an anchor element in each item that encloses two image elements – one scaled down and one full size
```
<dl id = "pix">
<dt><a><img src = "65vette.png" width="66"
                    height="40" alt="65 Thumbnail">
<img class = "hid" src="65vette.png" width="250"
                    height="150" alt="65 Vette"></a></dt>

<dt><a><img src = "67vette.png"  width="66"
                    height="40" alt="67 Thumbnail">
<img class = "hid" src="67vette.png" width="250"
                    height="150" alt="67 Vette"></a></dt>
</dl>
```

visibility.css

2   Save the HTML document then create a linked style sheet containing rules to position the list
```
dl#pix  { position : absolute ; top : 10px ; left : 10px }
```

3   Next add a style rule to position and hide the image elements containing the full-size images
```
dl#pix a img.hid { width : 250px ; height : 150px ; top : 0px ;
position : absolute ; left : 120px ; visibility : hidden }
```

4   Now add a style rule to reveal a full-size image element when the cursor is placed over its scaled-down version
```
dl#pix a:hover img.hid { visibility : visible }
```

5   Save the style sheet alongside the HTML document then open the web page in a browser and place the cursor over a scaled-down image to see its full-size version

Don't forget

Hidden elements still occupy space in the document – they just can't be seen.

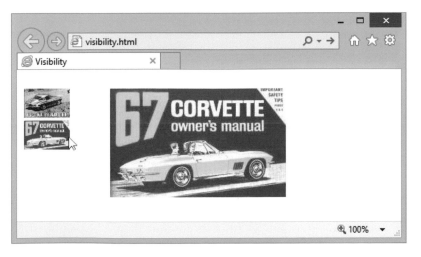

Summary

- CSS provides the four pseudo-elements :**before**, :**after**, :**first-letter**, and :**first-line**, that can enhance HTML content

- The **content** property can specify text to generate, or can accept the **open-quote** and **close-quote** keywords to generate quote marks

- Additionally non-text can be generated by specifying items within the parentheses of the **url()** or **attr()** keywords to the **content** property

- The **content** property may also generate automatic numbering by specifying the **counter()** keyword

- A **counter-increment** property can specify a counter name and increment value but may be reset by the **counter-reset** property

- The :**first-child** pseudo-class acts on the first selected element contained within an outer element

- Content languages can be identified by the :**lang()** pseudo-class

- The **cursor** property may specify a particular cursor to display using the cursor keywords or by stating the path to a cursor file within the parentheses of the **url()** keyword

- The **outline** property can specify the individual **outline-style**, **outline-width**, and **outline-color** properties as CSS shorthand

- Style can be applied to an interactive element that can receive user input by the :**focus** pseudo-class

- Hyperlink status can be indicated using the :**link**, :**visited**, :**hover**, and :**active** pseudo-classes

- Rollover effects with images, or on buttons and tabs, can also be achieved with :**link**, :**visited**, :**hover**, and :**active** pseudo-classes

- Setting the **display** property of an anchor element to **block** expands it to the boundaries of its containing element

- A selected element's **visibility** property may specify **hidden** or **visible** to determine whether its content should be displayed

Enhancing content

The chapter demonstrates CSS3 enhancement features that have standard support in all the latest web browsers.

Rounding corners

The appearance of content box borders can be enhanced by rounding their corners with the CSS3 **border-radius** property. Where all corners are to have the same radius this property can specify the radius size as a distance from the corner point in both horizontal and vertical directions. For example, as a value of **20px:**

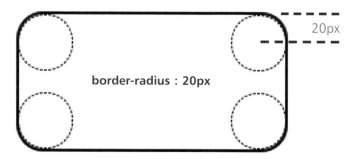

Individual corners may also be rounded by specifying a radius size to **border-top-left, border-top-right, border-bottom-right,** and **border-bottom-left** properties:

Don't forget

In older browsers that do not support the CSS3 **border-radius** property the rule will simply be ignored and the content box will be rectangular.

Alternatively, individual corners may be rounded by using **border-radius** as a shorthand property to specify four values – one value for each corner in the order **border-top-left, border-top-right, border-bottom-right, border-bottom-left.** Where a zero value is specified for any corner no radius will be produced. Individual corners may also be curved by specifying two values to define an ellipse so the horizontal and vertical directions get a different radius. The first value specifies the horizontal x radius and the second value specifies the vertical y radius. For example **border-top-right-radius : 20px 50px** defines an ellipse.

Circles can be created by setting the border-radius property to exactly half the size (including borders) of a square content box.

1 Create an HTML document with three div content boxes
```
<div id="box-1"><p>All Rounded Corners</p></div>
<div id="box-2"><p>Individual Corners</p></div>
<div id="box-3"><p>Circle</p></div>
```

radius.html

2 Save the HTML document then create a linked style sheet containing a rule to position the content boxes
```
div { float : left ; margin : 10px ; height : 120px ;
width : 120px ; border : 5px solid black ; text-align : center }
```

radius.css

3 Now add a rule to color the background and uniformly round all corners of the first content box
```
div#box-1 { background : yellow ; border-radius : 40px }
```

4 Next add a rule to color the background and individually round corners of the second content box
```
div#box-2 { background : lime ;
            border-top-left-radius : 50px ;
            border-bottom-right-radius : 50px }
```

5 Finally add a rule to color the background and make the third content box appear circular
```
div#box-3 { background-color : aqua ; border-radius: 65px }
```

6 Save the style sheet alongside the HTML document then open the web page in a browser to see the corners of the content boxes get rounded

Hot tip

The second content box in this example could alternatively be styled with a rule of **border-radius : 50px 0 50px 0**.

Casting shadows

The appearance of content boxes can be enhanced by adding drop-shadow effects with the CSS3 **box-shadow** property. Horizontal and vertical offset values must be specified to position the shadow. Where these are positive values the shadow will be positioned to the right and below the content box. Conversely negative values can be specified to position the shadow to the left and above respectively. For example, positive values of **20px 10px**:

Optionally the **box-shadow** property can have a third value to specify a blur distance that determines how blurred the shadow's edge will be – the higher the value, the more blurred. For example, a blur distance of **20px** expands the shadow to blur its edge in an area that is 10 pixels either side of the original offset:

Additionally a fourth optional value can specify a spread distance to determine how far the shadow should extend beyond the offset.

Although by default the shadow will be black, a color value should then be specified to explicitly set the shadow's color. Finally the **inset** keyword can optionally be used to create an inner shadow.

1 Create an HTML document with three div content boxes
```
<div id="box-1"> </div>
<div id="box-2"> </div>
<div id="box-3"> </div>
```

box-shadow.html

2 Save the HTML document then create a linked style sheet containing a rule to position the content boxes
```
div { float : left ; margin : 10px ; height : 120px ;
        width : 120px ; border : 5px solid black }
```

box-shadow.css

3 Now add a rule to create an outer drop shadow with 10 pixel offsets and a 10 pixel wide blur area on the first box
```
div#box-1 { box-shadow : 10px 10px 10px yellow }
```

4 Next add a rule to create an inner shadow with 10 pixel offsets and a 10 pixel wide blur area on the second box
```
div#box-2 { box-shadow : 10px 10px 10px lime inset }
```

5 Finally add a rule to create a glow effect with a 10 pixel wide blur and a 10 pixel wide spread on the third box
```
div#box-3 { box-shadow : 0 0 10px 10px aqua }
```

6 Save the style sheet alongside the HTML document then open the web page in a browser to see the shadow effects get added to the content boxes

Hot tip

Set both offsets to zero to create a "glow" effect – like the third content box in this example.

Shadowing text

The appearance of text can be enhanced by adding drop-shadow effects with the CSS3 **text-shadow** property. Horizontal and vertical offset values must be specified to position the shadow. Where these are positive values the shadow will be positioned to the right and below the text. Conversely, negative values can be specified to position the shadow to the left and above respectively. For example, positive values of **20px 10px:**

20px

10px

Optionally, the **text-shadow** property can have a third value to specify a blur distance that determines how blurred the shadow's edge will be – the higher the value, the more blurred. For example, a blur distance of **10px** expands the shadow to blur its edge in an area that is 5 pixels either side of the original offset:

25px

15px

Don't forget

As with the **box-shadow** property you should always explicitly specify a color to **text-shadow**.

Additionally, a fourth optional value can specify a spread distance to determine how far the shadow should extend beyond the offset.

Although by default the shadow will be black, a color value should then be specified to explicitly set its color.

1 Create an HTML document with three div content boxes
```
<div id="box-1"><p>CSS</p></div>
<div id="box-2"><p>HTML</p></div>
<div id="box-3"><p>PHP</p></div>
```

HTML

text-shadow.html

2 Save the HTML document then create a linked style sheet containing a rule to position the content boxes and specify a heavy font for centered text
```
div { float : left ; margin : 10px ; height : 120px ;
width : 120px ; border : 5px solid black ;
text-align : center ; font : 26pt "Arial Black" , cursive }
```

CSS

text-shadow.css

3 Now add a rule to color the text and create a black shadow with 3 pixel positive offsets plus a 4 pixel wide blur area for text in the first box
```
div#box-1 { color : yellow ; text-shadow : 3px 3px 4px black }
```

4 Next add a rule to color the text and create a black shadow with 3 pixel negative offsets plus a 4 pixel wide blur area for text in the second box
```
div#box-2 { color : lime ; text-shadow : -3px -3px 4px black }
```

5 Finally add a rule to create a glow effect with a 2 pixel wide blur and a 10 pixel wide spread on the third box
```
div#box-3 { color : black ; text-shadow : 0 0 2px 10px aqua }
```

6 Save the style sheet alongside the HTML document then open the web page in a browser to see the shadow effects get added to the text in the content boxes

Hot tip

As with **box-shadow,** set both offsets to zero to create a "glow" effect with **text-shadow**.

139

Making clear

The appearance of colors can be enhanced by adding transparency effects using the alpha channel of the CSS3 **rgba()** value specifier. This is similar to the **rgb()** value specifier, described on page 50, but additionally accepts a fourth value in the range **0.0** (fully transparent) to **1.0** (fully opaque). For example, to specify red with 50% transparency use **rgba(255 , 0 , 0 , 0.5)**.

CSS3 also allows color values to be specified in terms of Hue, Saturation, and Lightness with the **hsl()** color specifier. Saturation and Lightness are expressed as percentages. Hue is specified in the range 0-360, defining the color's position in degrees on a color wheel where Red is at 0 or 360, Green is at 120, and Blue is at 240 – with other colors at angles in between these points. For example, full red can be specified as **hsl(0 , 100% , 50%)**.

0

240   120

Hot tip

You can easily create matching shades with **hsl()** by keeping the same Hue value and varying the Saturation and Lightness values.

Transparency effects can also be applied using the alpha channel of the companion **hsla()** color specifier that accepts a fourth value in the range **0.0** (fully transparent) to **1.0** (fully opaque). For example, red with 50% transparency is **hsla(0 , 100% , 50% , 0.5)**.

Alternatively, transparency can be specified using the CSS3 **opacity** property with a value in the range **0.0** to **1.0**. This is similar to setting transparency with **rgba()** and **hsla()** but has one subtle difference – the **opacity** property value is inherited by the entire element. So text in an element with a background **opacity** of **0.5** will also be 50% transparent but if the background was made 50% transparent using the alpha channel of **rgba()** or **hsla()** the text would be fully opaque.

1 Create an HTML document with three div content boxes
```
<div id="box-1"><p>100% Opaque</p></div>
<div id="box-2"><p>50% Alpha</p></div>
<div id="box-3"><p>50% Opacity</p></div>
```

opacity.html

2 Save the HTML document then create a linked style sheet containing a rule to position the content boxes
```
div { float : left ; margin : 10px ; height : 120px ;
width : 120px ; border : 5px solid black ; text-align : center }
```

opacity.css

3 Now add a rule to color the background of the first content box with a fully-opaque yellow value
```
div#box-1 { background : rgb( 255 , 255 , 0 }
```

4 Next add a rule to color the background of the second content box with 50% yellow using the alpha channel
```
div#box-2 { background : rgba( 255 . 255 , 0 , 0.5 }
```

5 Finally add a rule to color the background of the third content box with 50% yellow using the **opacity** property
```
div#box-3 { background : rgb( 255, 255, 0 ) ; opacity : 0.5 }
```

6 Save the style sheet alongside the HTML document then open the web page in a browser to see the transparency effects get added differently to the content boxes

Hot tip

You can indicate that an element is disabled or inactive by using the opacity property.

141

Sizing backgrounds

The appearance of element backgrounds can be enhanced by controlling the background image size using the CSS3 **background-size** property. This allows images to be scaled and stretched by specifying two values for the image width and height. For example, to resize a 100-pixel square image to fill a 100 x 50px rectangle with **background-size: 100px 50px**. This scales down the image vertically to fill the element's height but maintains the image width.

Alternatively, percentage values can be specified to resize the background image. These determine what percentage of the element area should be covered. For example, to resize a 100-pixel square image to fill a 100 x 50px rectangle with **background-size: 100% 100%**. This again scales down the image vertically.

Additionally, the **background-size** property accepts keywords of **contain** or **cover** to control the image size. These scale the background image differently in respect of overflow. The **contain** keyword does not allow overflow, so scales the image to ensure both its width and height fit inside the element's content box. Conversely, the **cover** keyword does allow overflow, so scales the image to ensure it fills the largest side of the content box and automatically hides any overflowing part of the scaled image.

original

100 pixels x 100 pixels

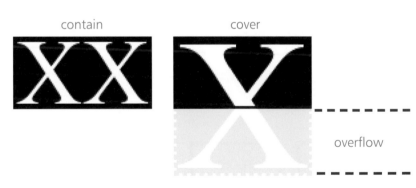

contain

cover

overflow

Specifying **background-size** values of **100% 100%** scales or stretches the background image to precisely fill the element's content box. Smaller percentages will, by default, see the image tiled – unless **background-repeat** is set to **no-repeat**. Larger percentages will see just a part of the image fill the element's entire content box.

1 Create an HTML document with three div content boxes
```
<div id="box-1"> </div>
<div id="box-2"> </div>
<div id="box-3"> </div>
```

background-size.html

2 Save the HTML document then create a linked style sheet containing a rule to position the content boxes and to specify a common background image
```
div {    float : left ; margin : 10px ; height : 120px ;
         width : 120px ; border : 5px solid black ;
         background :  url( flower.png ) }
```

background-size.css

3 Now add a rule to scale the background image size down to precisely fill the first content box
```
div#box-1 { background-size : 100%  100% }
```

4 Next add a rule to scale the background image size down to be a quarter of the background area – so it gets tiled to fill the second content box
```
div#box-2 { background-size : 50% 50% }
```

flower.png
300 pixels 300 pixels

5 Finally add a rule to scale the background image size down to be double that of the background area – so a quarter of the image fills the third content box
```
div#box-3 { background-size : 200% 200% }
```

6 Save the style sheet alongside the HTML document then open the web page in a browser to see the background image get resized to fill the content boxes

Beware

Optionally you can specify just one value to **background-size** and the second value is assumed to be **auto**. This is not the same as the first specified value though, so **50%** alone will not produce the same result as **50% 50%**.

143

Summary

- The appearance of content box borders can be enhanced by rounding their corners with the CSS3 **border-radius** property

- Individual corners can be rounded using **border-top-left**, **border-top-right**, **border-bottom-right**, and **border-bottom-left**

- The **border-radius** shorthand property can be used a to specify four values – one for each corner in the order **border-top-left**, **border-top-right**, **border-bottom-right**, **border-bottom-left**

- The appearance of content boxes can be enhanced by adding drop-shadow effects with the CSS3 **box-shadow** property to specify the shadow's position, blur, spread, and color

- Optionally the **inset** keyword can be specified to the **box-shadow** property to create an inner shadow

- The appearance of text can be enhanced by adding drop-shadow effects with the CSS3 **text-shadow** property to specify the shadow's position, blur, spread, and color

- Horizontal and vertical offset values must always be specified to the **box-shadow** and **text-shadow** properties

- The appearance of colors can be enhanced by adding transparency effects using the alpha channel of the CSS3 **rgba()** value specifier or the CSS3 **hsla()** value specifier

- Only transparency created with the CSS3 **opacity** property is inherited by the entire element

- The appearance of element backgrounds can be enhanced by controlling the background image size using the CSS3 **background-size** property

- The **background-size** property accepts length and percentage values or keywords **contain** or **cover** to control the image size

- Overflow is not allowed by the **contain** keyword but it is allowed and automatically hidden by the **cover** keyword

9 Looking ahead

The chapter demonstrates CSS3 features that have experimental support in some of the latest web browsers.

Bordering images

Web browser vendors introduce support for the latest CSS3 features by initially adding a prefix to the property name, which will be removed later when that feature becomes stable:

Prefix :	Browser :
-ms-	Internet Explorer
-moz-	Firefox
-webkit-	Google Chrome & Safari
-o-	Opera

This means that style sheets using features that currently have only experimental support, like all examples in this chapter, must have a separate rule with each vendor prefix. Additionally, to future-proof the style sheet there should also be an unprefixed version of the rule – anticipating removal of the prefix.

The experimental CSS3 **border-image** property allows a specified image to be drawn in the border of a content box. It requires three values stating the image location, what percentage of the image to display, and a keyword of **stretch**, **repeat**, or **round** defining how to apply the image to the border.

border-image.html

border-image.css

star.png
20px x 20px

1 Create an HTML document containing one content box
<div id="star">Border Image</div>

2 Save the HTML document then create a linked style sheet containing a rule to size and color the content box – and create a border area for a border image
**div#star { width : 480px ; height : 50px ;
background : aqua ; border : 20px solid transparent }**

3 Now add a rule attempting to apply an image to the border in each web browser
**div#star {
-ms-border-image : url(star.png) 100% repeat ;
-moz-border-image : url(star.png) 100% repeat ;
-webkit-border-image : url(star.png) 100% repeat ;
-o-border-image : url(star.png) 100% repeat ;
border-image : url(star.png) 100% repeat
}**

...cont'd

4 Save the style sheet alongside the HTML document then open the web page in various browsers to see if they yet support the experimental CSS3 **border-image** property

Hot tip

The **round** keyword means tile the image for as many times that a whole number fits into the border space.

Don't forget

Currently three of these browsers apply the image to the border corner but only Safari has implemented the repeat instruction.

Radiating gradients

CSS3 provides three properties to create gradient fills, which the browser blends smoothly from one specified color to another – **linear-gradient**, **repeating-linear-gradient** and **radial-gradient**.

The **linear-gradient** property creates the color transition along a linear path blending from one "color stop" point to another. Optionally its first value may be an angle, such as **45deg**. Each color stop may then be defined by a pair of values specifying a color and a position along the linear path. For example **red 50%**, **yellow 100%** defines color stops at the path's mid-point and end.

Similarly the **repeating-linear-gradient** property accepts exactly the same values as the **linear-gradient** property but automatically repeats the gradient after the last color stop has been reached.

The **radial-gradient** property also blends from one color stop to another but the path spreads out from a center point. By default it begins at the center of the element and is circular. Optionally the **ellipse** keyword can be specified along with length and position values to define a different radial shape and different center point.

Hot tip

You can also use keywords **to top bottom left right** to describe a linear path. For example, **to bottom right**.

gradient.html

gradient.css

1. Create an HTML document with three div content boxes
```
<div id="box-1"> </div>
<div id="box-2"> </div>
<div id="box-3"> </div>
```

2. Save the HTML document then create a linked style sheet containing a rule to position the content boxes
```
div { float : left ; margin : 10px ; height : 120px ;
            width : 120px ; border : 5px solid black }
```

3. Now add a rule to create a linear gradient fill in the background of the first content box
```
div#box-1 {
background : -ms-linear-gradient( 45deg, red 10% ,
                            yellow 70%, blue 90% ) ;
background : -moz-linear-gradient( 45deg, red 10% ,
                            yellow 70%, blue 90% ) ;
background : -webkit-linear-gradient( 45deg, red 10% ,
                            yellow 70%, blue 90% ) ;
background : -o-linear-gradient( 45deg, red 10% ,
                            yellow 70%, blue 90% ) ;
background : linear-gradient( 45deg, red 10% ,
                            yellow 70%, blue 90% ) }
```

4 Next add a rule to create a repeating linear gradient fill in the background of the second content box

```
div#box-2 {
background : -ms-repeating-linear-gradient( red 10%,
                              yellow 20%, blue 30% ) ;
background : -moz-repeating-linear-gradient( red 10%,
                              yellow 20%, blue 30% ) ;
background : -webkit-repeating-linear-gradient( red 10%,
                              yellow 20%, blue 30% ) ;
background : -o-repeating-linear-gradient( red 10%,
                              yellow 20%, blue 30% ) ;
background : repeating-linear-gradient( red 10%,
                              yellow 20%, blue 30% ) }
```

Don't forget

Each gradient must have at least two color stops.

5 Finally add a rule to create a repeating radial gradient fill in the background of the third content box

```
div#box-3{
background : -ms-radial-gradient( red 25% ,
                              yellow 50%, blue 75%  ) ;
background : -moz-radial-gradient( red 25% ,
                              yellow 50%, blue 75%  ) ;
background : -webkit-radial-gradient( red 25% ,
                              yellow 50%, blue 75%  ) ;
background : -o-radial-gradient( red 25% ,
                              yellow 50%, blue 75%  ) ;
background : radial-gradient( red 25% ,
                              yellow 50%, blue 75%  ) }
```

6 Save the style sheet alongside the HTML document then open the web page in a browser to see the gradient fills

Hot tip

You can specify the same color for the first and last color stops in a repeating gradient to avoid abrupt changes.

149

Writing columns

CSS3 can create a special content box that automatically displays its contents in columns. This is referred to as a "column box" and is created by specifying a desired column width, or an integer that is the number of desired columns, to a **columns** property.

Adjacent columns are separated by a gap that by default has a width value of **1em**. This can be modified by specifying an alternative width value to the **column-gap** property.

The gap between columns can also include a vertical ruled line if both columns contain content. Its appearance can be determined by specifying a width, style, and color to a **column-rule** property.

column-layout.html

column-layout.css

1　Create an HTML document with a single div element containing a heading and a paragraph of text
<div id="box"><h3>What is CSS?</h3><p>Cascading Style Sheets control the presentational aspects of HTML documents. CSS was created by the W3C to regain control of document markup. Websites designed with external CSS style sheets are easily maintained.</p></div>

2　Save the HTML document then create a linked style sheet containing a rule to position the element
div#box { float : left ; margin : 10px ; height : 120px ; width : 420px ; border : 5px solid black }

3　Add a rule to make the element into a column box with four columns
div#box {
-ms-columns : 4 ;
-moz-columns : 4 ;
-webkit-columns : 4 ;
-o-columns : 4 ;
columns : 4 }

4　Next add a rule to set the column gap to 10 pixels wide
div#box {
-ms-column-gap : 10px ;
-moz-column-gap : 10px ;
-webkit-column-gap : 10px ;
-o-column-gap : 10px ;
column-gap : 10px }

5 Now add a rule to display a red dashed ruled line between columns that both contain content
div#box {
-ms-column-rule : 3px dashed red ;
-moz-column-rule : 3px dashed red ;
-webkit-column-rule : 3px dashed red ;
-o-column-rule : 3px dashed red ;
column-rule : 3px dashed red }

6 Finally add a rule to specify how content that overflows the columns should be handled
div#box { overflow : hidden }

7 Save the style sheet alongside the HTML document then open the web page in a browser to see the text content get written into columns

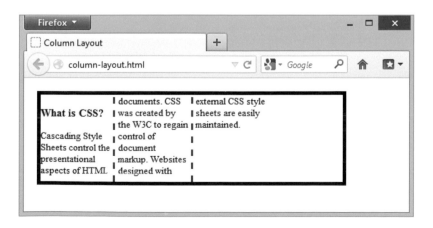

Hot tip

In some browsers you can control column breaks using **break-before**, **break-after**, and **break-inside** properties. For example try adding **div#box > p { break-before : column }** here.

Flexing boxes

CSS3 can allow content boxes to be flexible so they remain proportionately sized relative to each other when the dimensions of the containing element changes.

To create a flexible box ("flexbox") layout you must first create a flexbox container by setting the **display** property of an element that is to contain flexible content boxes with a **flexbox** value.

Content boxes within the flexbox container can then specify an integer value to their **flex** property to determine what proportion of available space they should occupy.

flexbox.html

flexbox.css

Beware

Notice how the property names differ even without vendor prefixes.

1 Create an HTML document with three div content boxes contained within a single outer div element
```
<div id="wrapper">
        <div id="box-1"><p>Flex=1</p></div>
        <div id="box-2"><p>Flex=2</p></div>
        <div id="box-3"><p>Flex=3</p></div>
</div>
```

2 Save the HTML document then create a linked style sheet containing a rule to size the outer div element
```
div#wrapper { height : 120px ; width : 95% ;
        border : 5px solid black ; text-align : center }
```

3 Add a rule to make the outer div element into a flexible box container – so its contained content boxes can flex
```
div#wrapper {
display : -ms-flexbox ;
display : -moz-box ;
display : -webkit-box ;
display : -o-flexbox ;
display : box ;
display : flexbox }
```

4 Now add a rule to specify a background color and flex proportion for the first contained content box
```
div#box-1 {
background : yellow ;
-ms-flex : 1 ;
-moz-box-flex : 1 ;
-webkit-box-flex : 1 ;
-o-flex : 1 ;
box-flex : 1 ;
flex : 1 }
```

5 Next add a rule to specify a background color and flex proportion for the second contained content box
div#box-2 { background : lime ; -ms-flex : 2 ; -o-flex : 2 ;
-moz-box-flex : 2 ; -webkit-box-flex : 2 ; box-flex : 2 ; flex : 2 }

6 Finally add a rule to specify a background color and flex proportion for the third contained content box
div#box-3{ background : aqua ; -ms-flex : 3 ; -o-flex : 3 ;
-moz-box-flex : 3 ; -webkit-box-flex : 3 ; box-flex : 3 ; flex : 3 }

7 Save the style sheet alongside the HTML document then open the web page in a browser to see the relative proportions of the contained content boxes

8 Enlarge the browser window to see the flexible boxes retain their proportions within their enlarged container

Laying grids

Building on the principle of flexible boxes in the previous example CSS3 can create a flexible grid of content boxes, arranged in rows and columns, that remain proportionately sized and relatively positioned when the size of the containing element changes.

To create a grid layout you must first create a grid container by setting the **display** property of an element that is to contain the content boxes with a **grid** value. The size of the columns and rows can then be specified to **grid-columns** and **grid-rows** properties. Their values may be lengths (**px**), percentages (**%**), or fractions (**fr**).

Content boxes are positioned in "tracks" within the grid using a 1-based index by specifying an integer value to their **grid-row** and **grid-column** properties. For example **grid-row : 1** is the top row. Additionally each content box can be made to span multiple rows or columns using **grid-column-span** and **grid-row-span** properties.

At the time of writing, this CSS3 feature is only supported by Internet Explorer so this example uses the **-ms-** vendor prefix.

Don't forget

HTML tables position content whereas CSS3 grids position elements.

grid.html

1. Create an HTML document with five div content boxes contained within a single outer div element
```
<div id="wrapper">
        <div id="box-1">Game Title</div>
        <div id="box-2">Stats</div>
        <div id="box-3">Score</div>
        <div id="box-4">Game Board</div>
        <div id="box-5">Controls</div>
</div>
```

grid.css

2. Save the HTML document then create a linked style sheet containing a rule to size the outer div element
```
div#wrapper { height : 120px ; width : 95% ;
        border : 2px solid black ; text-align : center }
```

3. Add a rule to make the outer div element into a grid container – so its contained content boxes can be arranged in tracks on 2 columns and 3 rows
```
div#wrapper {
display : -ms-grid ;
-ms-grid-columns : 25% 1fr ;
-ms-grid-rows: 25% 1fr 25% }
```

4 Now add rules to specify background colors and position 3 content boxes in the first column

div#box-1 { -ms-grid-column : 1 ; -ms-grid-row : 1 ;
background : yellow }
div#box-2 { -ms-grid-column : 1 ; -ms-grid-row : 2 ;
background : lime ; }
div#box-3 { -ms-grid-column : 1 ; -ms-grid-row : 3 ;
background : aqua }

5 Next add rules to position content boxes in the second column – with the first box spanning over 2 rows

div#box-4 { -ms-grid-column : 2 ; -ms-grid-row : 1 ;
-ms-grid-row-span : 2 ; background : orange }
div#box-5 { -ms-grid-column : 2 ; -ms-grid-row : 3 ;
background : fuchsia }

6 Save the style sheet alongside the HTML document then open the web page in a browser to see the grid layout and enlarge the browser window to see the grid maintained

Transforming shapes

CSS3 can dynamically manipulate content boxes to change their size, position, or orientation, by specifying one of the transformation functions below to their **transform** property:

Function :	Transform :
scale(n1,n2)	Scales X and Y axis all by the ratio *n1 n2*
scaleX(n)	Scales X axis by the ratio *n*
scaleY(n)	Scales Y axis by the ratio *n*
skew(n1,n2)	Scales X and Y axis all by the angle *n1 n2*
skewX(n)	Scales X axis by the angle *n*
skewY(n)	Scales Y axis by the angle *n*
rotate(n)	Rotates by the angle *n* amount
rotateX(n)	Rotates X axis by the angle *n* amount
rotateY(n)	Rotates Y axis by the angle *n* amount
translate(n1,n2)	Moves X and Y axis by *n1 n2* amount
translateX(n)	Moves X axis by *n* amount
translateY(n)	Moves Y axis by *n* amount

The transform can be specified to the element's **:active** pseudo-class so the transformation will be performed when the user makes it active, for instance by clicking on that element.

transform.html

transform.css

1. Create an HTML document with three div content boxes
```
<div id="box-1"> </div>
<div id="box-2"> </div>
<div id="box-3"> </div>
```

2. Save the HTML document then create a linked style sheet containing a rule to position the content boxes
```
div { float : left ; margin : 10px ; height : 120px ;
            width : 120px ; border : 5px solid black }
```

3. Add rules to specify the background of each content box
```
div#box-1 { background : yellow }
div#box-2 { background : lime }
div#box-3 { background : url( patch.png ) ;
                    background-size : 100% }
```

4 Now add a rule to rotate the first box when active
div#box-1:active { -ms-transform : rotate(45deg) ;
-moz-transform : rotate(45deg) ;
-webkit-transform : rotate(45deg) ;
-o-transform : rotate(45deg) ; transform : rotate(45deg) }

5 Next add a rule to scale the second box when active
div#box-2:active { -ms-transform : scale(0.5) ;
-moz-transform : scale(0.5) ;
-webkit-transform : scale(0.5) ;
-o-transform : scale(0.5) ; transform : scale(0.5) }

6 Finally add a rule to flip the third box when active
div#box-3:active { -ms-transform : rotateX(180deg) ;
-moz-transform : rotateX(180deg) ;
-webkit-transform : rotateX(180deg) ;
-o-transform : rotateX(180deg) ; transform : rotateX(180deg) }

7 Save the style sheet alongside the HTML document then
open the web page in a browser and click each box in
turn to see them transform

Hot tip

There is also a less
frequently used **matrix()**
transform function that
manipulates vector
notation values.

157

Making transitions

CSS3 can dynamically manipulate property values to change their color, size, position, orientation, etc over a specified period of time to create simple animated effects with the **transition** property.

The **transition** property specifies a **transition-duration** time value for the effect, such as **5s** for a five second duration, and one of the **transition-timing-function** calls below:

Function :	Transition :
linear	Consistent speed from start to end
ease	Increases from start to reach full speed then decreases at end (default)
ease-in	Increases at start only
ease-out	Decreases at end only
ease-in-out	Increases at start and decreases at end
steps	Between a number of intervals
cubic-bezier(*x1,y1,x2,y2*)	Elastic or bounce between coordinates

Additionally you can also specify a third **transition-delay** time value, such as **2s**, so the effect will not begin immediately.

The transition can be specified to an element's **:active** pseudo-class so the transformation will be performed when the user makes it active, for instance by clicking on that element, but will end abruptly unless it is also specified to its **:hover** pseudo-class.

transition.html

transition.css

1. Create an HTML document with two div content boxes
```
<div id="box-1"> </div>
<div id="box-2"> </div>
```

2. Save the HTML document then create a linked style sheet containing a rule to position the content boxes
```
div { float : left ; margin : 10px ; height : 120px ;
         width : 120px ; border : 5px solid black }
```

3. Add rules to color the background of each content box
```
div#box-1 { background : yellow }
div#box-2 { background : lime }
```

4 Now add a rule to change the background color of the first content box when it is in focus, with the cursor over
div#box-1:hover {
background : aqua ;
-ms-transition : 1s ease-in-out ;
-moz-transition : 1s ease-in-out ;
-webkit-transition : 1s ease-in-out ;
-o-transition : 1s ease-in-out ;
transition : 1s ease-in-out }

5 Next add a rule to change the shape of the second content box when it is made active, with a click
div#box-2:active {
border-radius : 65px ;
-ms-transition : 1s ease-in-out ;
-moz-transition : 1s ease-in-out ;
-webkit-transition : 1s ease-in-out ;
-o-transition : 1s ease-in-out ;
transition : 1s ease-in-out }

6 Finally add a rule to allow the transition to complete when it is made inactive, with the cursor remaining over
div#box-2:hover {
-ms-transition : 1s ease-in-out ;
-moz-transition : 1s ease-in-out ;
-webkit-transition : 1s ease-in-out ;
-o-transition : 1s ease-in-out ;
transition : 1s ease-in-out }

7 Save the style sheet alongside the HTML document then open the web page in a browser and position the cursor to see the transitions

Animating elements

CSS3 can dynamically manipulate property values over a specified period of time with the **transition** property, as described on the previous page, but can also nominate "keyframes" to determine property values at particular points for the **animation** property.

Keyframes are created by a CSS3 **@keyframes** ("at keyframes") rule that defines an animation name and selects points using **from** and **to** keywords, and one or more percentages. For example, naming an animation "bounce" and selecting three points like this:
@keyframes bounce {
from { top : 100px } 50% { top : 200px } to { top : 300px } }

The **animation** property can specify, in this order, the animation name (defined by the **@keyframes** rule), duration, timing function, delay, iteration count, and direction. Timing functions are the same as those for transitions, such as **ease-in-out**, and the iteration count may be an integer or the keyword **infinite**. Interestingly, the direction can be specified as **normal** (the default), **reverse**, or **alternate** – alternating between playing forward and reverse on successive iterations.

animation.html

animation.css

1 Create an HTML document with three div content boxes
```
<div id="box-1"> </div>
<div id="box-2"> </div>
<div id="box-3"> </div>
```

2 Save the HTML document then create a linked style sheet containing a rule to absolutely position the top of the content boxes
```
div { position : absolute ; top : 10px ; height : 120px ;
      width : 120px ; border : 5px solid black }
```

3 Add rules to color the background and position the left of each content box – making the third box circular and stacked above the first box
```
div#box-1 { background : yellow ; left : 50px ; z-index : 1 }
div#box-2 { background : lime ; left : 400px ; z-index : 1 }
div#box-3 {
background-color : aqua ;
left: 50px ;
border-radius : 65px ;
z-index : 2 }
```

4 Now define an animation named "slide" to move between the left positions of the square content boxes

```
@-ms-keyframes slide {
              from { left : 50px } to { left : 400px } }
@-moz-keyframes slide {
              from { left : 50px } to { left : 400px } }
@-webkit-keyframes slide {
              from { left : 50px } to { left : 400px } }
@-o-keyframes slide {
              from { left : 50px } to { left : 400px } }
@keyframes slide {
              from { left : 50px } to { left : 400px } }
```

5 Next add a rule to animate the circular content box by repeatedly sliding it over the two other boxes

```
div#box-3 {
-ms-animation : slide 3s alternate infinite ;
-moz-animation : slide 3s alternate infinite ;
-webkit-animation : slide 3s alternate infinite ;
-o-animation : slide 3s alternate infinite ;
animation : slide 3s alternate infinite }
```

6 Save the style sheet alongside the HTML document then open the web page in a browser to see the animation

Hot tip

The **from** keyword can alternatively be written as **0%** and the **to** keyword can alternatively be written as **100%**.

Hyphenating text

CSS3 enables the automatic hyphenation of text according to a built-in dictionary with the **hyphens** property. This can specify a value of **auto** to turn on automatic hyphenation or a **manual** value to allow hyphenation only when suggested by a hyphen character or soft hyphen, such as the **­** HTML entity.

Additionally CSS3 provides further properties for precise hyphenation control. The amount of unfilled space, before text justification, that can be left in a line before hyphenation occurs can be specified as a length to a **hyphenate-limit-zone** property. For example **hyphenate-limit-zone : 50px** allows 50 pixels of space. The minimum number of characters permissible in a hyphenated word can be specified to a **hyphenate-limit-chars** property. Similarly the maximum number of permissible consecutive hyphenated lines in an element can be specified to a **hyphenate-limit-lines** property.

Although seemingly trivial, hyphenation control can have a significant effect on the appearance of text content.

hyphen.html

1 Create an HTML document with two div content boxes containing identical text
<div id=" box-1">The Brooklyn Bridge in New York City spans the East River to connect the boroughs of Manhattan and Brooklyn. Upon its completion in 1883 it was the longest suspension bridge in the world and the first steel-wire suspension bridge.</div>

<div id="box-2">The Brooklyn Bridge in New York City spans the East River to connect the boroughs of Manhattan and Brooklyn. Upon its completion in 1883 it was the longest suspension bridge in the world and the first steel-wire suspension bridge.</div>

hyphen.css

2 Save the HTML document then create a linked style sheet containing a rule to position the content boxes
**div { float : left ; margin : 20px ;
                                    height : 200px ; width : 200px }**

3 Add rules to color the background of the content boxes
div#box-1 { background : aqua }
div#box-2 { background : yellow }

4 Now add a rule to justify the text in both content boxes and ensure that any overflow will be visible
div {
text-align : justify ;
overflow : visible }

5 Next add a rule to turn on automatic hyphenation in the second content box
div#box-2 {
-ms-hyphens : auto ;
-moz-hyphens : auto ;
-webkit-hyphens : auto ;
-o-hyphens : auto ;
hyphens : auto }

6 Save the style sheet alongside the HTML document then open the web page in a browser to see how the text appearance differs with automatic hyphenation

Hot tip

Hyphenation is especially useful with the column layout demonstrated on page 150.

163

The Brooklyn Bridge in New York City spans the East River to connect the boroughs of Manhattan and Brooklyn. Upon its completion in 1883 it was the longest suspension bridge in the world and the first steel wire suspension bridge.

The Brooklyn Bridge in New York City spans the East River to connect the boroughs of Manhattan and Brooklyn. Upon its completion in 1883 it was the longest suspension bridge in the world and the first steel-wire suspension bridge.

Flowing regions

CSS3 enables data to be streamed from a specified source HTML document into regions of a second "host" HTML document. This allows the creation of layouts similar to those seen in magazines where content surrounds unrelated items such as advertisements.

The data must first be made accessible to the host document by assigning the URL of the source document to the **src** attribute of an **<iframe>** element in the host – so it acts as a data container.

In the host document's style sheet a rule can then select the **<iframe>** and a data-flow name of your choice can be specified to a **flow-into** property. The data can now be streamed into one or more selected regions of the host document by specifying your chosen data-flow name to a **flow-from** property.

When streaming data into multiple regions it is logical to use a common class identity for each regional element. Styles applied to the source document are maintained in the streamed data.

Don't forget

Specifying a **flow-into** property on an **<iframe>** sets its **display** property to **none** – so it will never be visible.

data-source.html

data-source.css

1 Create an HTML document to act as a data source
   <div><span id="car">Lamborghini Aventador</span> sets new benchmarks in the sports car segment.<img src="aventador.png">Revolutionary Italian design goes far beyond what was previously thought possible.</div>

2 Save the HTML source document then create a linked style sheet containing a rule to style the spanned text
   span#car { color : red ; font-style : italic }

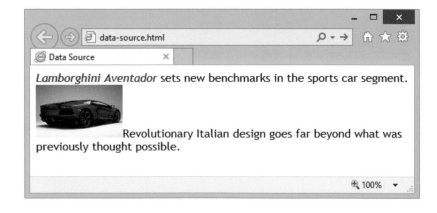

3 Now create an HTML document to act as a host – containing a data container and three div content boxes as regions with a common class identity

region.html

```
<iframe id="data" src="data-source.html">
[Data container]
</iframe>
<div id="box-1" class="region"></div>
<div id="box-2" class="region"></div>
<div id="box-3" class="region"></div>
```

4 Save the host document then create a linked style sheet containing a rule to position the content boxes

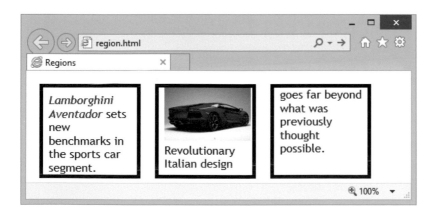

region.css

```
div { float : left ; margin : 10px ; height : 120px ; width : 130px ; border : 5px solid black ; overflow : hidden }
```

5 Next add a rule to establish a data-flow named "f1"

```
iframe#data { -ms-flow-into : f1 ; -moz-flow-into : f1 ; -webkit-flow-into : f1 ; -o-flow-into: f1 ; flow-into : f1 }
```

6 Finally add a rule to flow the data into the content box regions of the host document

```
div.region { -ms-flow-from : f1 ; -moz-flow-from : f1 ; -webkit-flow-from : f1 ; -o-flow-from : f1 ; flow-from : f1 }
```

7 Save the style sheet alongside the HTML document then open both web pages in a browser to see how source data flows into host regions and maintains applied styles

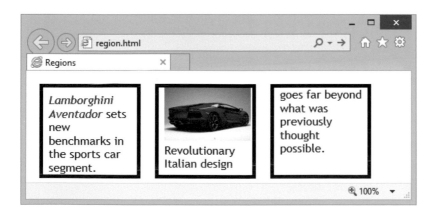

Excluding shapes

CSS3 enables text to wrap so it can completely surround elements – whereas the **float** property, demonstrated on page 68, simply allows a content box to be positioned at the left or right boundary of its containing element.

A surrounded element is excluded from the normal flow of content and is created using a **wrap-flow** property that can specify how content should wrap around it using one of these keywords:

Keyword :	Wraps :
both	Content flows on all sides of the exclusion
start	Content flows on the left side only
end	Content flows on the right side only
clear	Content flows on top and bottom only

Additionally an offset distance can be specified to a **wrap-margin** property to create a margin space around an excluded element.

exclude.html

1 Create an HTML document with two div content boxes that each contain text
<div id="box-1">Cascading Style Sheets are used to control the presentational aspects of HTML documents. It was created by the W3C to regain control of document markup. Websites designed with external CSS style sheets are more easily maintained than those using internal style sheets as the style code is centralized. CSS reduces website file sizes for faster downloading.</div>

<div id="box-2">What Is CSS?</div>

exclude.css

2 Save the HTML document then create a linked style sheet containing a rule to size the first content box, justify its text content, and hide any overflow
**div#box-1 {
height : 130px ;
width : 480px ;
border : 5px solid black ;
overflow : hidden ;
text-align : justify }**

3 Now add a rule to absolutely position the second content box and to set its background color

```
div#box-2 {
position : absolute ; top : 60px ; left : 200px ;
padding : 5px ;
border : 1px dashed black ; background : yellow }
```

4 Next add a rule to make the second content box an excluded element that allows content flow on all sides

```
div#box-2 {
-ms-wrap-flow : both ;
-moz-wrap-flow : both ;
-webkit-wrap-flow : both ;
-o-wrap-flow : both ;
wrap-flow : both }
```

5 Finally add a rule to create a 10 pixel wide margin around the excluded element

```
div#box-2 {
-ms-wrap-margin : 10px ;
-moz-wrap-margin : 10px ;
-webkit-wrap-margin : 10px ;
-o-wrap-margin : 10px ;
wrap-margin : 10px }
```

6 Save the style sheet alongside the HTML document then open the web page in a browser to see content flow around the excluded content box

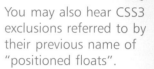

Hot tip

You may also hear CSS3 exclusions referred to by their previous name of "positioned floats".

167

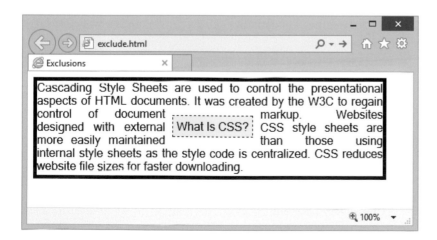

Summary

- Style sheets that include vendor-prefixed CSS3 properties can be future-proofed by also including an unprefixed version

- An image may be drawn in the border of a content box by the **border-image** property

- Gradient fills can be created using the **linear-gradient, repeating-linear-gradient** and **radial-gradient** properties

- Column boxes that display content in columns are created by the **columns, column-gap,** and **column-rule** properties

- A flexible box layout is created by setting a container element's **display** property and its child element's **flex** property

- A grid layout is created by setting a container element's **display, grid-rows,** and **grid-columns** properties

- Content boxes are positioned within a grid by **grid-row, grid-column, grid-row-span,** and **grid-column-span** properties

- The **scale(), skew(), rotate(),** and **translate()** functions can be specified to the **transform** property for dynamic manipulation

- Simple animation is created by specifying a **transition-duration** and **transition-timing-function** to the **transition** property

- Keyframes are created by an **@keyframes** rule to determine property values at particular points for the **animation** property

- Automatic hyphenation can be turned on by specifying an **auto** value to the **hyphens** property of an element

- An HTML **<iframe>** element can be used as a data container

- Data can be streamed from a data container into a named data-flow by the **flow-into** property, then from there into regions of a document by the **flow-from** property

- An exclusion element that allows content to wrap around it is created by the **wrap-flow** and **wrap-margin** properties

10 Following guidelines

This chaper demonstrates established best practices that have been adopted by style sheet authors.

Resetting browser defaults

Cascading Style Sheets give the web designer powerful control over every aspect of the page content but it must be remembered that each browser has default values that will be applied to elements in the absence of CSS style rule for those elements. This can cause inconsistencies in the appearance of the page design across different browsers so it is important to reset the browser's default values to ensure that the style sheet has total control of the design so it will appear the same in different browsers.

A commonly-seen reset using the universal selector looks like this:

* { margin : 0 ; padding : 0 }

This rigorously resets the margin and padding areas to zero on every single element in the document but is not the best reset technique because it is heavy on the browser's rendering engine.

To reset the browser's default values the style rules should select each element to be reset and specify how they should be reset.

Hot tip

The reset style rules in this example are based upon the Yahoo! UI Library – further details can be found online at **http://developer.yahoo. com/yui/cssreset**.

reset.css

1 Create a reset style sheet with a rule to set page colors
html { color : black ; background : white }

2 Next add a style rule to explicitly set element margin and padding areas to zero
body,div,dl,dt,dd,ul,ol,li,h1,h2,h3,h4,h5,h6,pre,form, fieldset,legend,input,textarea,p,blockquote,th,td { margin : 0 ; padding : 0 }

3 Now add style rules to remove element borders
table { border-collapse : collapse ; border-spacing : 0 } fieldset,img,abbr,acronym { border : 0 }

4 Then add style rules to set the font appearance
address,caption,cite,code,dfn,em,strong,th,var { font-style : normal ; font-weight : normal } h1,h2,h3,h4,h5,h6 { font-size : 100% ; font-weight : normal }

5 Now add style rules to remove list markers and to left-align text content
ol,ul { list-style : none } caption,th,td { text-align : left }

6 Finally, add style rules to control other elements
```
q:before,q:after { content : " " }
abbr,acronym { border : 0 ; font-variant : normal }
sup { vertical-align : text-top }
sub { vertical-align : text-bottom }
input,textarea,select { font-family : inherit ;
font-size : inherit ; font-weight : inherit }
input,textarea,select { * font-size : 100% }
legend { color : #000 }
```

7 Save the style sheet as "reset.css" for inclusion at the beginning of all your other style sheets to reset the browser default styles before other rules are applied

8 Create another style sheet that begins by resetting the browser's default style values
```
@import "reset.css" ;
```

neutral.css

9 Save the second style sheet alongside the first one then create an HTML document, linked to the second style sheet
```
<h1>Large Heading</h1><h3>Small Heading</h3>
<ol><li>One<li>Two<li>Three</ol>
<table><caption>Table</caption>
<tr><td>One</td><td>Two</td><td>Three</td></tr>
</table>
```

neutral.html

10 Save the HTML document alongside the style sheets then open the web page in a browser to see how the default broswer styles have been removed

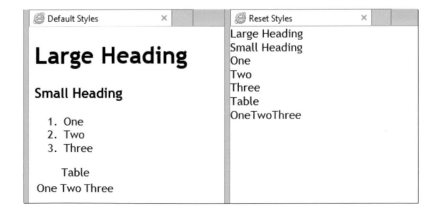

Organizing your code

Modular style sheets

When styling large websites it is useful to make individual style sheets for different purposes and then link them in a single master style sheet. For example, maintain browser reset styles, typographic styles, and structure styles independently in different style sheets then link them together in a master style sheet, like this:

```
@import "reset.css" ;
@import "structure.css" ;
@import "typography.css" ;
```

Hot tip

The **@import** directive can optionally use the **url()** keyword, such as @import url("reset.css"); but it's not essential.

Describing sections

Each style sheet should ideally be separated into sections with commented headings describing the purpose of that section. This makes the code easier for others to understand and easier for you to understand when revisiting the code some time later. For example, describing a navigation panel section:

```
/*********************************/

/* Primary Navigation - Top Links */

/*********************************/

div#nav {
border : 0.5em solid red ;
margin : 1em auto ;
padding : 0.2em
}
```

Code consistency

Some style sheet authors like to list the rule declarations in alphabetical property order to more readily find a declaration – like those listed in the code section above. Additionally, it is good practice to omit the terminating semi-colon after the final declaration but some style sheet authors prefer to include it so further declarations can be simply appended at a later date. The general rule of thumb when writing style rules is to place the declarations on separate lines when there are more than three declarations, otherwise place them on a single line. Above all it is recommended you adopt your preferred style of writing style sheets and use it consistently.

1 Create a simple HTML document containing one heading and one paragraph

```
<h1>CSS Code</h1>
<p>Style sheets should be organized for readability!</p>
```

code.html

2 Save the HTML document then create a linked style sheet beginning with a descriptive header

```
/*
Description: Tabloid newspaper format.
Author: Mike McGrath
Version: 1.0
*/
```

code.css

3 Next add a directive to reset the browser default styles

```
/* Reset browser defaults. */
@import "reset.css" ;
```

4 Now add a single-line rule for the paragraph content

```
/* Text content. */
p { font : large cursive  }
```

5 Finally add a multi-line alphabetically-arranged rule for the heading element

```
/* Banner headings. */
h1 {
background : red ;
color : white ;
font : 2em white ;
padding: 0.2em ;
width : 5em }
```

6 Save the style sheet alongside the HTML document then open the web page in a browser to see the rules applied

Don't forget

Remember to add a terminating semi-colon after each **@import** directive.

173

Optimizing style rules

Inheriting values

In order to optimize style sheet code it's important to recognize that many property values of a parent element are inherited by the child element it contains. Most commonly the **font** and **color** properties are inherited from the containing parent element. So if a style rule sets these properties for the parent element a further rule need not repeat them for the child element – unless different values are desired. For example:

div { font-size : 2em ; color : red }
div.hello { font-size : 2em ; color : blue }

can be written more efficiently as:

div { font-size : 2em ; color : red }
div.hello { color : blue }

Sizing text

When specifying text size it is best practice to avoid absolute unit values in order to allow the user to enlarge text. The preferred method is to size text relative to the browser using **em** units. Standard browser font size is **1em**, which is equal to **16px**. A little web designer trick is to reset the font size with this style rule:

body { font-size : 62.5% }

This sets **1em = 10px** so where, for example, an **18px** text size is desired a rule declaration of **font-size : 1.8em** can be specified without the need to calculate the **em** size.

Employing shorthand

Always use CSS shorthand properties rather than individual properties to keep style sheet code concise. For example:

margin-left : 2px ;
margin-top : 3px ;
margin-right : 4px ;
margin-bottom : 5px ;

can be written more efficiently as:

margin : 3px 4px 5px 2px ;

Similarly, use shorthand for **border, background, padding, font** and other properties. Additionally, with color values represented by three pairs of hexadecimal digits its value can be specified more efficiently by omitting every second digit like this:

#ff3366 can be written as: **#f36**.

1. Create an HTML document with a single paragraph containing two sections of spanned text

```
<p>
Optimized text with <br><span>inherited values</span>
<br>and also <span id="mod">overriding values</span>
</p>
```

optimum.html

2. Save the HTML document then create a linked style sheet with a directive to reset the default browser styles

```
/* Reset browser defaults. */
@import "reset.css" ;
```

optimum.css

3. Next add a style rule to reset the font

```
/* Reset the font so that 1em=10px. */
body { font-size : 62.5% }
```

4. Now add a style rule to set text size and color

```
/* Set the text size to 18px and color. */
p { font-size : 1.8em ; color : red }
```

5. Then add a style rule to override an inherited value

```
/* Override inherited color value. */
span#mod { color : blue }
```

6. Finally add a style rule to set borders with shorthand

```
/* Set borders using shorthand. */
p { border : 3px dashed #0f0 }
```

7. Save the style sheet alongside the HTML document then open the web page in a browser to see the optimum styles

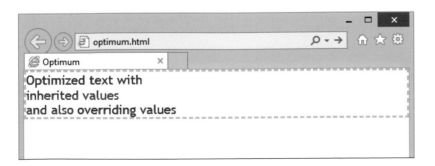

Employing multiple classes

An HTML element's **class** attribute can be assigned multiple values, each separated by a space. This is a very powerful feature of CSS, allowing you to apply styles from more than one class to any element.

classes.html

1 Create an HTML document containing six paragraphs that each include a class attribute

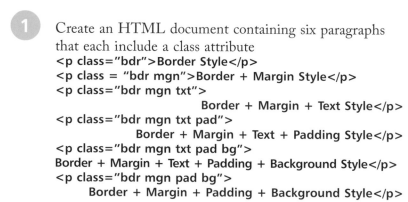

```
<p class="bdr">Border Style</p>
<p class = "bdr mgn">Border + Margin Style</p>
<p class="bdr mgn txt">
                              Border + Margin + Text Style</p>
<p class="bdr mgn txt pad">
                 Border + Margin + Text + Padding Style</p>
<p class="bdr mgn txt pad bg">
Border + Margin + Text + Padding + Background Style</p>
<p class="bdr mgn pad bg">
        Border + Margin + Padding + Background Style</p>
```

classes.css

2 Save the HTML document then create a linked style sheet with a directive to reset the default browser styles

```
/* Reset browser defaults. */
@import "reset.css" ;
```

3 Next add a style rule for a border class

```
/* Border style. */
p.bdr { border : 5px outset red }
```

4 Now add a style rule for a margin class

```
/* Margin size. */
p.mgn { margin : 1em }
```

5 Then add a style rule for a text class

```
/* Text style. */
p.txt { font : 2em fantasy }
```

6 Now add a style rule for a padding class

```
/* Padding. */
p.pad { padding : 0.5em }
```

7 Finally add a style rule for a background class

```
/* Background. */
p.bg { background : yellow }
```

8 Save the style sheet alongside the HTML document then open the web page in a browser to see the various class styles applied to the paragraphs

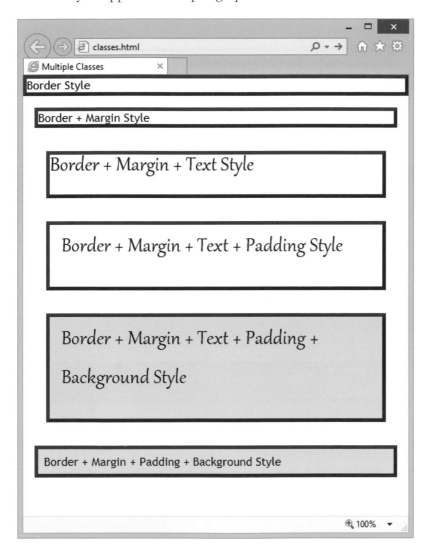

In the browser window:

Border Style

Border + Margin Style

Border + Margin + Text Style

Border + Margin + Text + Padding Style

Border + Margin + Text + Padding + Background Style

Border + Margin + Padding + Background Style

Don't forget

Notice that the margin width increases when the text size is increased because the margin width value is specified as a relative **em** value.

177

Hot tip

Typically, when using multiple classes, each style rule will only define one or two properties.

Validating style sheets

Web browsers make no attempt to validate code so it's well worth verifying every HTML document and CSS style sheet before the web page is published, even when the page looks fine in your browser. When the browser encounters code errors it makes a guess at what is intended – but different browsers may make different interpretations and so display the page incorrectly. The World Wide Web Consortium (W3C) provides free online validator tools that check web page code for errors.

The W3C is the recognized body that oversees standards on the web. See the latest developments on its informative website at **www.w3.org**.

1. Create an HTML document and a linked CSS style sheet

2. With an internet connection, open a web browser and navigate to the W3C HTML Validator Tool at **http://validator.w3.org** then click the "Validate by File Upload" tab and select your HTML document

3. Now click the "Check" button to upload a copy of your file then see the test result appear

Hot tip

Other tabs in the HTML Validator allow you to enter the web address of an online document to validate or copy and paste code for validation.

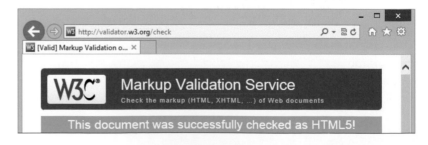

4 Next navigate to the W3C CSS Validator Tool at **http://jigsaw.w3.org/css-validator/** then click the "By file upload" tab and select your CSS style sheet

5 Now click the "Check" button to upload a copy of your file then see the test result appear

If validation fails the errors are listed so you may easily correct them. When validation succeeds you may choose to include a W3C CSS validation icon at the end of the HTML document.

Hot tip

Always validate the HTML document code before validating its CSS linked style sheets.

Don't forget

The W3C icons can also act as hyperlinks to their respective validators for easy online validation.

Compressing code files

Lengthy CSS style sheets can be streamlined for faster download time by "minification" to preserve the operational qualities of the code while reducing its overall byte footprint. The minification process removes comments, unnecessary whitespace, and line breaks.

One of the best minification tools is the YUI Compressor that is part of the Yahoo! UI Library and is freely available for download at **http://developer.yahoo.com/yui/compressor**. This application is written in Java, so requires Java version 1.4 or later to be installed on your computer.

1 With Java installed, download the YUI Compressor and place the **yuicompressor-x.x.x.jar** file on your desktop

2 Next copy the style sheet to be minified to your desktop, say the "reset.css" file described earlier

Hot tip

The YUI Compressor can also be used to minify JavaScript code files.

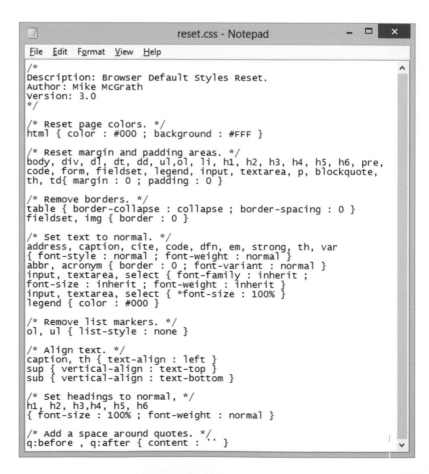

```
                           reset.css - Notepad        –  □   ×

File  Edit  Format  View  Help
/*
Description: Browser Default Styles Reset.
Author: Mike McGrath
Version: 3.0
*/

/* Reset page colors. */
html { color : #000 ; background : #FFF }

/* Reset margin and padding areas. */
body, div, dl, dt, dd, ul,ol, li, h1, h2, h3, h4, h5, h6, pre,
code, form, fieldset, legend, input, textarea, p, blockquote,
th, td{ margin : 0 ; padding : 0 }

/* Remove borders. */
table { border-collapse : collapse ; border-spacing : 0 }
fieldset, img { border : 0 }

/* Set text to normal. */
address, caption, cite, code, dfn, em, strong, th, var
{ font-style : normal ; font-weight : normal }
abbr, acronym { border : 0 ; font-variant : normal }
input, textarea, select { font-family : inherit ;
font-size : inherit ; font-weight : inherit }
input, textarea, select { *font-size : 100% }
legend { color : #000 }

/* Remove list markers. */
ol, ul { list-style : none }

/* Align text. */
caption, th { text-align : left }
sup { vertical-align : text-top }
sub { vertical-align : text-bottom }

/* Set headings to normal, */
h1, h2, h3,h4, h5, h6
{ font-size : 100% ; font-weight : normal }

/* Add a space around quotes. */
q:before , q:after { content : '' }
```

3 Insert a ! character after the opening /* of any comments you wish to keep, e.g. the heading, then save the changes

4 Now open a Command Prompt window then use the **cd** command to navigate to your desktop

5 At the Command Prompt issue the following command to minify the style sheet and overwrite the existing file, replacing **x.x.x** with the version number of your download **java -jar yuicompressor-x.x.x.jar reset.css -o reset.css**

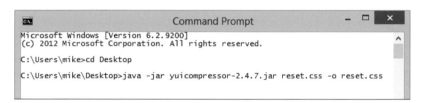

Hot tip

The command in this example states the input and output files as the same name to overwrite the original file with the minified output but a different output file name could be used to preserve the original file.

6 When the operation completes, open the style sheet in a plain text editor to see the minified code with the heading comment preserved

Hot tip

Add a **-v** option before the input file name in the command to see verbose output from the YUI Compressor advising of any errors.

Comparing the file size of the original and minified versions of the style sheet in this example reduced the original from 1,198 bytes to 767 bytes – about one third less. Of course this is just a small example but the savings can be considerable on larger, heavily-commented, style sheet files.

Summary

- Default styles may vary between browsers so it is best to always reset the browser defaults to ensure the style sheet has control

- A browser reset should select each element to be reset and specify how they should be reset

- Modular style sheets can be created for different aspects of a web site then incorporated in a single master style sheet

- Each style sheet should ideally be separated into sections with commented headings describing the purpose of that section

- Style rule declarations can be listed in alphabetical property order to readily find any declaration

- You may omit the terminating semi-colon after the final declaration in a style rule as it is superfluous

- Place style rules with fewer than four declarations on a single line, otherwise place them on multiple lines

- Do not repeatedly specify style rules for property values inherited from a parent element

- Avoid absolute units when specifying text size and use relative **em** units instead so that the user can enlarge text

- Always use CSS shorthand properties rather than individual properties to keep style sheet code concise

- Multiple classes can be assigned to an HTML element's **class** attribute to apply styles from more than one CSS class

- All HTML documents and CSS style sheets can be validated by the W3C online validation tools

- Style sheet file sizes can be reduced by minification to remove comments, unnecessary whitespace, and line breaks

11 Customizing pages

This chapter demonstrates how to apply multiple style sheets to a single web page for user choice and to suit different devices.

Recognizing media

CSS can provide different style sheets to allow the user to choose a preferred layout style and produce layouts appropriate for various situations. Adding a **media** attribute to the HTML **<link>** tag can specify a style sheet to be used for all devices with the **all** keyword, or specify style sheets for viewing on computer screens with the **screen** keyword. Other style sheets can be specified for mobile devices, such as cellphones, with the **handheld** keyword. Additionally, a style sheet for printer output can be specified with the **print** keyword, which will typically remove navigation links and advertising.

custom.html

Notice that alternative style sheets for viewing this web page on a computer screen are specified by assigning a value of "alternate stylesheet" to the HTML **rel** attribute.

1 Create an HTML document that specifies a variety of style sheets in its head section

```
<link rel="stylesheet" type="text/css" media="screen"
                       href="screen.css" title="Default Style">
<link rel="alternate stylesheet" type="text/css"
media="screen" href="reverse.css"
                           title="Reverse Color Style">
<link rel="alternate stylesheet" type="text/css"
media="screen" href="large.css" title="Large Text Style">
<link rel="alternate stylesheet" type="text/css"
media="screen" href="legacy.css" title="Simple Text Style">
<link rel="stylesheet" type="text/css" media="handheld"
        href="handheld.css" title="Mobile Device Style">
<link rel="stylesheet" type="text/css" media="print"
                       href="print.css" title="Printer Style">
```

2 Now add content within "div" elements in the body section

```
<div id="wrapper">
<div id="head"><h1>Cascading Style Sheets...</h1>
</div><div id="list">
<ul><li>Screen<li>Reverse<li>Large<li>Legacy
<li>Handheld<li>Print</ul></div>
<div id="tips"><h3>W3C</h3>The World Wide Web
Consortium oversees web standards.
<h3>XSL</h3>The eXtensible Stylesheet Language is less
popular than CSS.</div>
<div id="content"><h2>What is CSS?</h2>Cascading
Style Sheets are used to control the presentational aspects
of HTML documents. It was created by the World Wide
Web consortium to regain control of document markup.
Websites designed with external CSS style sheets are more
easily maintained than those using internal style sheets as
the style code is centralized. CSS reduces website file sizes
for faster downloading and provides precision control over
web page presentation.</div></div>
<div id="foot">Styled by CSS in easy steps</div>
```

Save the HTML document then open the web page in a browser to see how the content appears with the web browser's default styles

Cascading Style Sheets...

- Screen
- Reverse
- Large
- Legacy
- Handheld
- Print

W3C

The World Wide Web Consortium oversees web standards.

XSL

The eXtensible Stylesheet Language is less popular than CSS.

What is CSS?

Cascading Style Sheets are used to control the presentational aspects of HTML documents. It was created by the World Wide Web consortium to regain control of document markup. Websites designed with external CSS style sheets are more easily maintained than those using internal style sheets as the style code is centralized. CSS reduces website file sizes for faster downloading and provides precision control over web page presentation.
Styled by CSS in easy steps

Don't forget

Style sheets to format this basic HTML document are described throughout the rest of this chapter.

Adding page structure

The simple HTML document created on the previous page can be structured in several ways by CSS style sheets. Typically, regular web browsers can present its content as a familiar 3-column layout with a header and footer area, as described on page 72. Browser default styles should first be reset, as described on page 170.

screen.css

1. Create a linked style sheet for the HTML document created on the previous page with a directive to initially reset the default browser styles
@import "reset.css";

2. Next add another directive to execute style rules that structure the HTML document's elements
@import "structure.css";

structure.css

3. Save the style sheet alongside the HTML document then create a new style sheet with rules to ensure the document occupies the full height of the browser window
html, body { height : 100% }

   div#wrapper {
   min-height : 100% ;
   height : auto !important ;
   margin : 0 auto -30px }

4. Now add style rules to set the height of the header and footer areas
div#head { height : 60px }
div#foot { height : 30px }

5. Then add style rules to specify the column sizes
div#list { float : left ; width : 100px ; margin-left : 1.5em }
div#tips { float : right ; width : 100px }
div#content { margin : 0 120px }

6. Save the style sheet alongside the HTML document then open the web page in a browser to see the content appear in a 3-column structure with a header and footer area

Hot tip

The browser knows to use these style sheets in a web browser because it recognizes the media as "screen" from the **media** attribute in the **<link>** element.

Specifying default styles

The structured HTML document content described on the previous page can be stylized by adding rules to the default style sheet used by the browser for the screen media. If necessary the style sheet can explicitly be selected by choosing the name assigned to the **title** attribute in the **<link>** tag. In this example the name given is simply "Default Style".

screen.css

1 Edit the style sheet from the previous page by adding a rule to specify the overall background and text color
body { background : url(drops.png) white ; color : black }

2 Now add style rules to determine the appearance of each heading element
h1 { font : 2em sans-serif ; color : red }
h2 { color : blue ; font : 1.2em "Script", cursive }
h3 { background : red ; color : white }

3 Next add a style rule to specify how the list markers should appear
ul { list-style : url(tick.png) square ; margin-left : 10px }

4 Then add a style rule to set the font for text within the main content area
div#content { font : 1em sans-serif }

5 Finally add a style rule to determine how the footer area should appear
div#foot {
text-align : center; background : blue ; color : white }

6 Save the style sheet alongside the HTML document then open the web page in a browser to see the structured document appear with color, image, and font styles

7 Open the browser's style sheet dialog (with Internet Explorer 10 click Page, Style or View, Style on the Command bar) and note that the name assigned to the **<link>** element's **title** attribute is currently selected

Don't forget

Always specify an alternative style in case images are not available – here the alternatives are a white background and square list markers.

Specifying reverse styles

Alternate styling for the default styling described on the previous page can be made available to the user by creating another style sheet specified as "alternate stylesheet" to the **<link>** tag's **rel** attribute. Mostly web page styling employs black text on a white or pale background as it resembles the familiar format found in books and magazines. A colorful alternative can be provided using white or pale text on a colored background – reversing the typical format. To apply alternate styling the user simply chooses the name assigned to the **<link>** element's **title** attribute from the browser's style sheet dialog.

reverse.css

1   Create a new style sheet with directives to once again reset the browser's default styling and structure the content in a 3-column layout with header and footer areas
@import "reset.css" ;
@import "structure.css" ;

2   Next add a style rule to determine the overall background and text color
body { background : blue ; color : white }

3   Now add style rules to determine the appearance of each heading element
h1 { font : 2em sans-serif ; color : aqua }
h2 { color : aqua ; font : 1.2em "Script", cursive }
h3 { background : aqua ; color : black }

4   Next add a style rule to specify how the list markers should appear
ul { list-style : square ; margin-left : 10px }

5   Then add style rule to set the font for text within the main content area and footer area
div#content { font : 1em sans-serif }
div#foot { text-align : center ;
                                    background : aqua ; color : black }

6   Save the style sheet alongside the HTML document then open the web page in a browser and select the alternate style sheet name in the dialog to apply the reverse styles

Beware

Avoid colored backgrounds for pages that the user is likely to print out – unless a separate style sheet for printers is specified, as described on page 198-199.

Improving readability

Another alternative layout to those described on the previous pages provides a version especially for low-vision (partially-sighted) users. Typically this will feature larger text and a linear layout where elements are stacked on top of each other vertically.

Headings may have inverted colors and often content will employ yellow text on a black background as partially-sighted people find these easiest to read. Additionally, some elements may be removed to clarify the page content.

large.css

1. Create a new style sheet with a directive to once again reset the browser's default styling
@import "reset.css" ;

2. Next add a style rule to determine the overall background, text size and color
html { font : bold large sans-serif ;
background : black ; color : yellow }

3. Now add a style rule to determine the appearance of each heading element
h1, h2, h3 { background : yellow ; color : black }

4. Finally add style rules to generate parentheses around the footer text
div#foot:before { content : "(" }
div#foot:after { content : ")" }

5. Save the style sheet alongside the HTML document then open the web page in a browser and select the alternate style sheet name in the dialog to apply low-vision styles

Other popular colors for low-vision web pages are white text on a navy background.

Reverting to legacy styles

The examples in this book demonstrate Cascading Style Sheets, level 3, which is built on Cascading Style Sheets level 1 and 2 – so style sheets created for CSS1 also work in browsers that support CSS3. Additionally, style sheets created for CSS3 can be loaded in older "legacy" browsers that only support CSS1 and the browser will ignore elements and properties it doesn't recognize.

There are some interesting differences between CSS1 and CSS3 – positioning in CSS3 is more flexible and offers more options to the designer. Automated content allows developers to force the browser to display specific content elements as well as control the layout, look, and feel. Also there is support for special cursors and dynamic outlining in CSS3.

An alternate style sheet to those described on the previous pages can be provided for those users with older legacy browsers that only support CSS1.

legacy.css

1 Create a new style sheet with a rule to determine the generic text font style
body { font-family : sans-serif }

2 Now add style rules to determine the color of each heading element
h1 { color : red }
h2 { color : green }
h3 { color : blue }

3 Save the style sheet alongside the HTML document then open the web page in a browser and select the alternate style sheet name in the dialog to apply CSS1 styles

Don't forget

Legacy browsers may not support the **@import** directive so the browser reset is omitted here.

Providing handheld styles

Besides providing a variety of style sheets for viewing a page on a computer screen, a style sheet can be created to determine how the page should appear on a handheld device, such as a cellphone.

For handheld devices the **<link>** element's **media** attribute should be assigned the **handheld** keyword, and its **title** attribute omitted.

When designing page layouts for viewing on handheld devices consideration should be given to the device limitations. For example, multi-column layouts should be avoided due to the tiny screens on handheld devices (typically 100-320 pixels wide), in favor of a single-column layout. Also unnecessary information should be suppressed to speed page load times – especially the removal of advertising and images.

The clean simple layout suited to handheld devices is often also suitable for projected presentations, which can be identified by assigning the **projection** keyword to the **<link>** element's **media** attribute. Additionally multiple types can be assigned to this attribute as a comma-separated list, so the same style sheet can be specified for both handheld devices and projection with the attibute **media="handheld , projection"**.

handheld.css

1. Create a new style sheet with a directive to once again reset the browser's default styling
@import "reset.css" ;

2. Next add a style rule to specify the background and color of headings – to differentiate them from content text without using large fonts
h2 { background : red ; color : white }

3. Now add style rules to suppress unnecessary information – leaving just the actual content and its heading
div#list, div#foot, div#tips, h1, h3 { display : none }

4. Save the style sheet alongside the HTML document then open the web page in a browser on a handheld device, or via a projector, to see the simplified document

Scroll

Beware

Handheld devices often display content inconsistently – tables and CSS positioning are particulary troublesome.

Don't forget

With this example the browser retains the heading at the top of the screen when the user scrolls down the content.

Setting printer styles

Just as it is desirable to suppress some page items for display on handheld devices, as demonstrated in the previous example, it is often desirable to suppress items when printing pages.

For the printed page the **<link>** element's **media** attribute should be assigned the **print** keyword, and its **title** attribute omitted.

Where a color print is not required all color style rules can be removed in the print style sheet and prominence given to fonts.

When a print style sheet is defined the web browser will continue to display the page using the screen style sheet but will apply the print style sheet rules when sending the page to the printer. The print version can be seen with the browser's print preview feature.

print.css

1. Create a new style sheet with a rule to specify a uniform monospace font
body { font-family : monospace }

2. Now add a style rule to suppress unnecessary information – leaving just content and headings
div#foot, div#list { display : none }

3. Save the style sheet alongside the HTML document then open the web page in a browser and open the Print Preview to see the print style sheet rules get applied

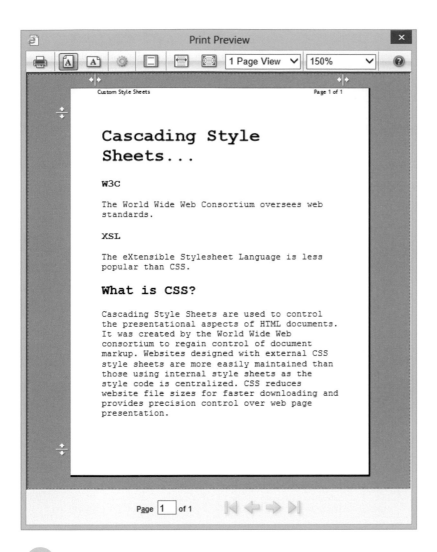

Cascading Style Sheets...

W3C

The World Wide Web Consortium oversees web standards.

XSL

The eXtensible Stylesheet Language is less popular than CSS.

What is CSS?

Cascading Style Sheets are used to control the presentational aspects of HTML documents. It was created by the World Wide Web consortium to regain control of document markup. Websites designed with external CSS style sheets are more easily maintained than those using internal style sheets as the style code is centralized. CSS reduces website file sizes for faster downloading and provides precision control over web page presentation.

Don't forget

Always provide a print media style sheet to make a web page more user-friendly – with colors, unnecessary images and advertising removed or suppressed.

4 Finally select File, Print on the browser menu to send the page to your printer and see the print appear with the print style rules applied

Summary

- CSS can provide different style sheets that allow the user to choose a preferred style and layout for various situations

- The HTML **<link>** element can include a **media** attribute that can be assigned the **all** keyword to specify a style sheet to be used for all devices

- Specifying a **screen** value to the **media** attribute designates a style sheet to be used only when viewed on a computer screen

- An **@import** directive can be used to include browser reset and layout structure style sheets within a master style sheet

- The HTML **<link>** element can include a **title** attribute with an assigned name that the user can select to use that style sheet

- Assigning a value of "alternate stylesheet" to the HTML **<link>** tag's **rel** attribute allows alternative style sheets to be specified for viewing on a computer screen

- The default style sheet will typically produce black content on a white background but a popular alternative style sheet will reverse this to produce white content on a dark background

- Style sheets for low-vision users typically arrange the content in a single-column layout with larger yellow text on a black background, as partially-sighted people find this easiest to read

- Old legacy browsers that only support CSS1 will display parts of CSS3 style sheets that they recognize and ignore all others

- Positioning in CSS1 is less flexible than in CSS3 so an alternative style sheet can be provided for legacy browsers

- Specifying a **handheld** value to the **media** attribute designates a style sheet to be used when viewed on a mobile device

- Specifying a **print** value to the **media** attribute designates a style sheet to be used when the page gets printed, and its appearance can be viewed in the browser's Print Preview

12 Handy reference

This section of the book lists all of the established visual CSS properties and values.

Properties and values

The tables in this section list by name each visual CSS property and its possible Values. Each CSS property can be applied to any HTML element unless specific target elements are given in the table. For instance, a **border-collapse** property can only be applied to table and inline-table elements, whereas a **background** property can be applied to any element.

Property :	Values :
animation	*animation-delay* | *animation-direction* | *animation-duration* | *animation-iteration-count* | *animation-name* | *animation-timing-function*
animation-delay	*time*
animation-direction	**normal** | **alternate**
animation-duration	*time*
animation-iteration-count	*number* | **inherit**
animation-name	*name* | **none**
animation-timing-function	**ease** | **linear** | **ease-in** | **ease-out** | **ease-in-out** | **cubic-bezier(** *number, number, number, number* **)**
background	*background-attachment* | *background-color* | *background-image* | *background-origin* | *background-position* | *background-repeat* | *background-size* | **inherit**
background-attachment	**scroll** | **fixed** | **inherit**
background-color	*color* | **transparent** | **inherit**
background-image	*url* | **none** | **inherit**
background-origin	**border-box** | **padding-box** | **content-box**
background-position	**top left** | **top center** | **top right** | **center left** | **center center** | **center right** | **bottom left** | **bottom center** | **bottom right** | *x-% y-%* | *x-position y-position* | **inherit**
background-repeat	**repeat** | **repeat-x** | **repeat-y** | **no-repeat** | **inherit**
background-size	*length* | *percentage* | **auto** | **cover** | **contain**
border-collapse (table and inline-table elements)	**collapse** | **separate** | **inherit**
border-spacing (table and inline-table elements)	*length length?* | **inherit**

Property :	Values :
border	*border-width* | *border-style* | *border-color* | **inherit**
border-top border-right border-bottom border-left	*border-width* | *border-style* | *border-color* | **inherit**
border-color	*color* | **transparent** | **inherit**
border-top-color border-right-color border-bottom-color border-left-color	*color* | **transparent** | **inherit**
border-style	**none** | **hidden** | **dotted** | **dashed** | **solid** | **double** | **groove** | **ridge** | **inset** | **outset** | **inherit**
border-top-style border-right-style border-bottom-style border-left-style	**none** | **hidden** | **dotted** | **dashed** | **solid** | **double** | **groove** | **ridge** | **inset** | **outset** | **inherit**
border-width	**thin** | **medium** | **thick** | *length* | **inherit**
border-top-width border-right-width border-bottom-width border-left-width	**thin** | **medium** | **thick** | *length* | **inherit**
border-image	**url(** *url* **)** *percentage* **stretch** | **repeat** | **round** | **none**
border-radius	*border-top-right-radius* | *border-bottom-right-radius* | *border-bottom-left-radius* | *border-top-left-radius*
border-top-right-radius border-bottom-right-radius border-bottom-left-radius border-top-left-radius	*length*
bottom (positioned elements)	*length* | *percentage* | **auto** | **inherit**
box-flex	*number*
box-shadow	**inset** | *length, length, length, length* | *color* | **none**
caption-side (table caption elements)	**left** | **right** | **top** | **bottom** | **inherit**
clear (block-level elements)	**left** | **right** | **both** | **none** | **inherit**

...cont'd

Property :	Values :
clip (absolutely positioned elements)	rect(*top* , *right* , *bottom* , *left*) | **auto** | **inherit**
color	*color* | **inherit**
column-count	**auto** | *number*
column-gap	**normal** | *length*
column-rule	*column-rule-width* | *column-rule-style* | *column-rule-color*
column-rule-color	*color*
column-rule-style	*border-style*
column-rule-width	**thin** | **medium** | **thick** | *length*
columns	*column-width* | *column-count*
column-width	**auto** | *length*
content (:before and :after pseudo elements)	[*string* | *url* | *counter* | **attr(** *identifier* **)** | **open-quote** | **close-quote** | **no-open-quote** | **no-close-quote**]+ | **normal** | **inherit**
counter-increment	[*identifier-integer ?*]+ | **none** | **inherit**
counter-reset	[*identifier-integer ?*]+ | **none** | **inherit**
cursor	[[*url* ,]* | **auto** | **default** | **pointer** | **crosshair** | **move** | **e-resize** | **w-resize** | **n-resize** | **ne-resize** | **nw-resize** | **s-resize** | **se-resize** | **sw-resize** | **text** | **wait** | **help** | **progress**] | **inherit**
direction	**ltr** | **rtl** | **inherit**
display	**none** | **inline** | **block** | **inline-block** | **list-item** | **run-in** | **table** | **inline-table** | **table-row-group** | **table-header-group** | **table-footer-group** | **table-row** | **table-column-group** | **table-column** | **table-cell** | **table-caption** | **flexbox** | **grid** |**inherit**
empty-cells (table cell elements)	**show** | **hide** | **inherit**
float	**left** | **right** | **none** | **inherit**
font (may include optional values marked ?)	[[*font-style* | *font-variant* | *font-weight*]? *font-size* [/ *line-height*]? | *font-family*] | **caption** | **icon** | **menu** | **message-box** | **small-caption** | **status-bar** | **inherit**

Property :	Values :
font-family (may include optional values marked ?)	[[*family-name* | *generic-family*] ,]* [*family-name* | *generic-family*] | **inherit**
font-size	**xx-small** | **x-small** | **small** | **medium** | **large** | **x-large** | **xx-large** | **smaller** | **larger** | *length* | *percentage* | **inherit**
font-style	**italic** | **oblique** | **normal** | **inherit**
font-variant	**small-caps** | **normal** | **inherit**
font-weight	**normal** | **bold** | **bolder** | **lighter** | **inherit** | **100** | **200** | **300** | **400** | **500** | **600** | **700** | **800** | **900**
height (block-level and replaced elements)	*length* | *percentage* | **auto** | **inherit**
left (positioned elements)	*length* | *percentage* | **auto** | **inherit**
letter-spacing	*length* | **normal** | **inherit**
line-height	*length* | *percentage* | *number* | **normal** | **inherit**
list-style (elements whose display property has a **list-item value**)	[*list-style-type* | *list-style-image* | *list-style-position*] | **inherit**
list-style-image (elements whose display property has a **list-item** value)	*url* | **none** | **inherit**
list-style-position (elements whose display property has a **list-item** value)	**inside** | **outside** | **inherit**
list-style-type (elements whose display property has a **list-item** value)	**asterisks** | **box** | **check** | **circle** | **diamond** | **disc** | **hyphen** | **square** | **decimal** | **decimal-leading-zero** | **lower-roman** | **upper-roman** | **lower-alpha** | **upper-alpha** | **lower-greek** | **lower-latin** | **upper-latin** | **armenian** | **georgian** | **hebrew** | **hiragana** | **katakana** | **footnotes** | **none**
margin	*length* | *percentage* | **auto** | **inherit**
margin-top **margin-right** **margin-bottom** **margin-left**	*length* | *percentage* | **auto** | **inherit**

...cont'd

Property :	Values :
max-height	*length* | *percentage* | **none** | **inherit**
min-height	*length* | *percentage* | **inherit**
opacity	*number* | **inherit**
outline	*outline-color* | *outline-style* | *outline-width* | **inherit**
outline-color	*color* | **invert** | **inherit**
outline-offset	*length* | **inherit**
outline-style	**none** | **dotted** | **dashed** | **solid** | **double** | **groove** | **ridge** | **inset** | **outset** | **inherit**
outline-width	**thin** | **medium** | **thick** | *length* | **inherit**
overflow (applies to block-level and replaced elements)	**visible** | **hidden** | **scroll** | **auto** | **no-display** | **no-content** | *overflow-x* | *overflow-y* | **inherit**
overflow-x overflow-y	**visible** | **hidden** | **scroll** | **auto** | **no-display** | **no-content** | **inherit**
padding	*length* | *percentage* | **inherit**
padding-top padding-right padding-bottom padding-left	*length* | *percentage* | **inherit**
position	**static** | **relative** | **absolute** | **fixed** | **inherit**
quotes	[*string string*]+ | **none** | **inherit**
right (positioned elements)	*length* | *percentage* | **auto** | **inherit**
table-layout (table and inline-table elements)	**auto** | **fixed** | **inherit**
text-align (block-level elements)	**left** | **center** | **right** | **justify** | **inherit**
text-decoration	**underline** | **overline** | **line-through** | **blink** | **none** | **inherit**
text-indent (block-level elements)	*length* | *percentage* | **inherit**
text-justify	**auto** | **inter-word** | **inter-ideograph** | **inter-cluster** | **distribute** | **kashida** | **tibetan**
text-shadow	*length* | *color* | **none**

Property :	Values :
text-transform	uppercase | lowercase | capitalize | none | inherit
top (positioned elements)	*length* | *percentage* | auto | inherit
transform	scale | scale3d | scaleX | scaleY | scaleZ | rotate | rotate3d | rotateX | rotateY | rotateZ | skew | skewX | skewY | perspective | none
transform-origin	[*length* | *percentage* | left | center | right] [*length* | *percentage* | top | center | bottom] [*length*]
transition	*transition-property transition-duration transition-delay transition-timing-function*
transition-delay	*time*
transition-duration	*time*
transition-property	all | none
transition-timing-function	ease | linear | ease-in | ease-out | ease-in-out | cubic-Bezier(*number, number, number, number*)
unicode-bidi	normal | embed | bidi-override | inherit
vertical-align (inline elements and table cells)	baseline | sub | super | top | middle | bottom | text-top | text-bottom | *length* | *percentage* | inherit
visibility	visible | hidden | collapse | inherit
white-space	normal | nowrap | pre | pre-wrap | pre-line | inherit
width (block-level and replaced elements)	*length* | *percentage* | auto | inherit
word-break	normal | keep-all | loose | break-strict | break-all
word-spacing	normal | *length* | inherit
word-wrap	normal | break-word
z-index (positioned elements)	auto | *integer* | inherit

Selectors

Name :	Targets :	Example :
Universal	Any element	* { color : green }
Type	Any element of the specified type	p { color : green }
Grouping	Multiple elements of the specified types	h1, h2, h3 { color : green }
Class	The name assigned to a class attribute using dot notation	p.grn { color : green }
ID	The name assigned to an id attribute using hash notation	p#grn { color : green }
Descendant	An element that is a descendant of another specified element at any level, such as child or grandchild	div li { color : green }
Child	An element that is the direct child descendant of another specified element	div > p { color : green }
Adjacent sibling	An element that immediately follows another specified element in the document tree hierarchy	h3 + p { color : green }
General sibling	All elements that share the same specified parent element	h1 ~ p { color : green }
Attribute	Any element that includes the specified attribute	a[href] { color : green }
Attribute value	An element that includes a specified attribute that has been assigned a specified value	a[href="home"] { color : green }
Listed attribute value	An element that includes a specified attribute and value in a space-separated list of values	span[class~="grn"] { color : green }
Partial attribute value	An element that includes a specified attribute whose value contains a specified substring	span[lang="es"] { color : green }

Pseudo-classes

Class :	Targets :
:active	An activated element
:focus	An element that has focus
:visited	A link that has been visited
:hover	An element when the cursor rolls over it
:disabled	An element that is not enabled
:enabled	An element that is not disabled
:selection	An element that is currently selected by the user
:lang	An element with content of a specified language
:nth-child(*n*)	An element that is the nth sibling
:nth-last-child(*n*)	An element that is the nth sibling from the end
:first-child	An element that is the first sibling
:last-child	An element that is the final sibling
:only-child	An element that is the only child
:nth-of-type(*n*)	An element that is the nth sibling of its type
:nth-last-of-type(*n*)	An element that is the nth sibling of its type from the end
:first-of-type	An element that is the first sibling of its type
:last-of-type	An element that is the last sibling of its type
:only-of-type	An element that is the only child of its type
:empty	An element that has no children
:root	An element that is the top of the document tree
:not(*x*)	An element that is not represented by argument x

Pseudo-elements

Name :	Generates :	Example :
:before	A pseudo-element to insert content before all other content contained in a specified element	p:before { content : "[" }
after:	A pseudo-element to insert content after all other content contained in a specified element	p:after { content : "]" }
:first-letter	A pseudo-element to style the very first letter of content contained in a specified element	p:first-letter { font-size : larger }
:first-line	A pseudo-element to style the very first line of text content contained in a specified element	p:first-line { color : green }

Units

Name :	Measure :
%	Percentages
cm	Centimeters
in	Inches
mm	Millimeters
pc	Picas (1pc=12pt)
pt	Points (1pt=1/72 inch)
em	Current font size (1em)
ex	Height of lowercase x (1ex)
px	Pixels of the viewing device
deg	Degrees
s	Seconds
ms	Milliseconds

Index

213

U

V

W

X

Z